THE IMPERFECT INDIVIDUAL

WHY OUR WORLD IS IN TURMOIL AND HOW YOU CAN SAVE IT

DAVID COFFEY

authorHOUSE

AuthorHouse™ UK
1663 Liberty Drive
Bloomington, IN 47403 USA
www.authorhouse.co.uk
Phone: UK TFN: 0800 0148641 (Toll Free inside the UK)
*   UK Local: (02) 0369 56322 (+44 20 3695 6322 from outside the UK)*

Published by AuthorHouse 09/28/2022

ISBN: 978-1-7283-7463-5 (sc)
ISBN: 978-1-7283-7464-2 (e)

Print information available on the last page.

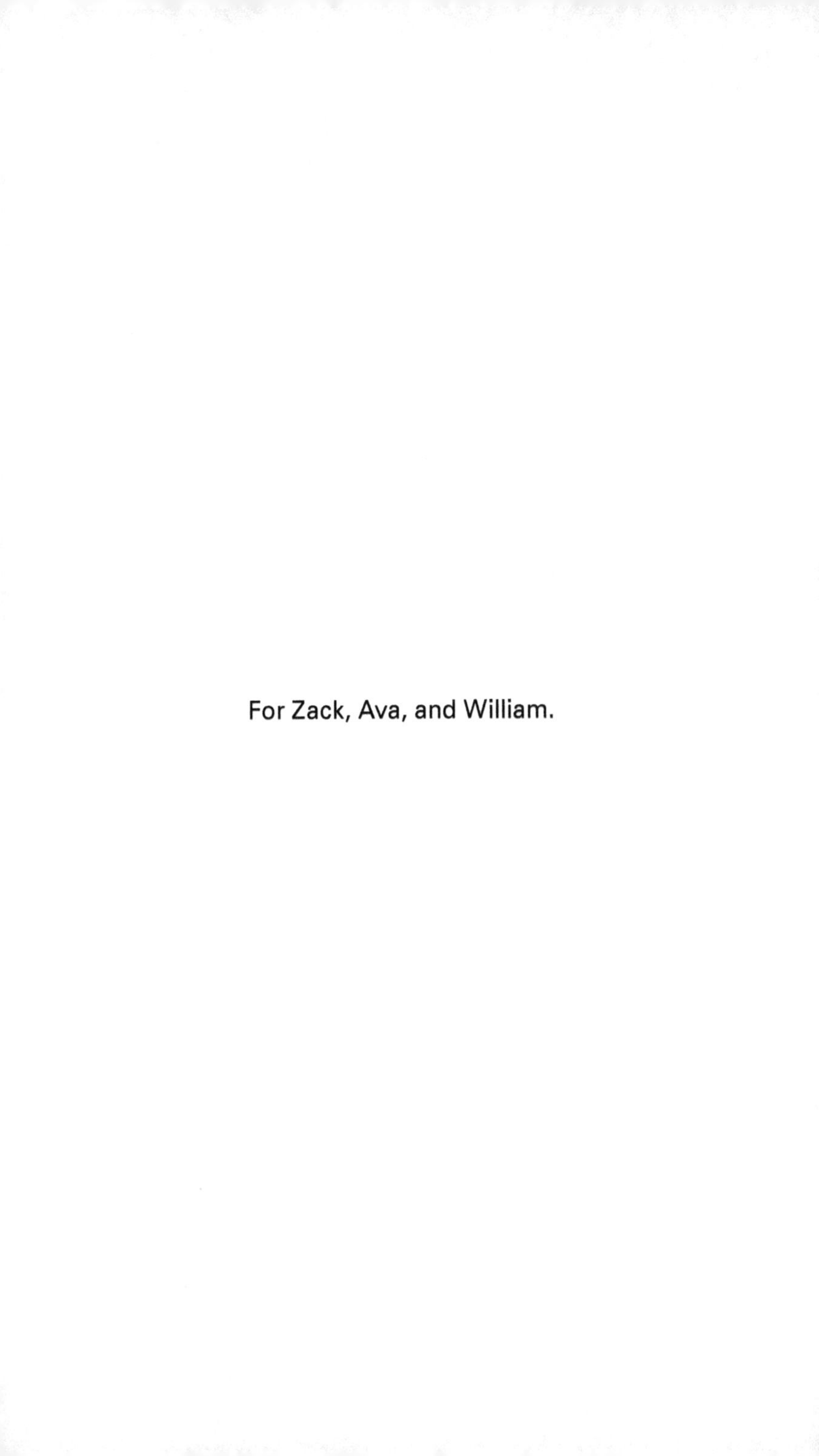

For Zack, Ava, and William.

*I looked upon the lilies
When the morning sun was low,
And the sun shone through a lily
With a softened honey glow.
A spot was in the lily
That moved incessantly,
And when I looked into the cup
I saw a morning bee.*

*"Consider the lilies!"
But, it occurs to me,
Does any one consider
The lily and the bee?*

*The lily stands for beauty,
Use, purity, and trust,
It does a four-fold duty,
As all good mortals must.
Its whiteness is to teach us,
Its faith to set us free,
Its beauty is to cheer us,
And its wealth is for the bee.*

*"Consider the lilies!"
But, it occurs to me,
Does any one consider
The lily and the bee?*

- The Lily And The Bee by Henry Lawson

In memory of all across the world who have died or been harmed as a result of lockdowns and COVID injections. We will not stop fighting for you.

Contents

Preface

'Someone call me ASAP.'

Four words, sent by my brother Chris on the family WhatsApp group at 19.53 on Monday, 18 October, that propelled me from the world I thought I was beginning to make some sense of into a brutal and terrifying new reality.

I instinctively just knew. Something had happened to my dad. He was gone. Less than one hour later, it was confirmed. My dad, who was on holiday in Poland with my brother, had collapsed in a restaurant and died. The day before, he had flown to Poland from the UK. The day before that, he had been administered a third COVID-19 'vaccine'.

I was with my dad prior to him going on holiday. We watched our team, Everton, play. Everton were losing 1–0 with about five minutes to go when my dad left for the airport. I stood at the door and watched him slowly walk away. He then walked back to put his foot on the doorstep to tie his shoelace before turning away once more and ambling down the road. I had a strange and horrible feeling that it would be the last time I would ever see him again. A premonition. A knowing.

At its deepest essence, this book explores life and death and Western society's strange and fearful approach to both. I try to ascertain why it is that so many millions have seemingly accepted a drab and largely meaningless existence in an effort to delay their own mortality, and why intuition and spirituality have been sacrificed at the altar of decadence, complacency, and ignorance. Why, indeed, have so many forgotten what it is to actually live?

My dad was a major influence in my life when he was alive, and since his passing, his values of humility, tolerance, loyalty, and duty shine even brighter as a guiding light for me in my life. He also had a zest for travel, exploration, and people, embracing all of the joys and opportunities that life offers whilst also refusing to be cowed by fear and threats, real or imagined. Life for my dad, in stark contrast to so many in the West today, really was about living.

Six days after he passed, I was out walking when a lone sycamore seed floated down and nestled itself in my coat pocket. A billion to one chance. I later discovered that the sycamore tree symbolises protection, divinity, eternity, and strength. My dad had sent me a message reassuring me that in this fractured, paranoid, and tyrannical world, I was needed, and that despite the trauma and overwhelming sense of grief, the candle of liberty, courage, and hope still burns.

I write this preface in July 2022, a time when the world is at a critical juncture and where each citizen bears a historic responsibility. Sickeningly, I observe that many of those citizens are not only becoming increasingly tolerant of evil but also propagating and even actively encouraging it. Yet there are also many who, having long ago chosen their hill to die on, will bear the torch of freedom and humanitarianism for present and future generations. These are the people who, like my dad, will be remembered as the bringers of light.

And so as we stand on the cusp of a new age, it is we who get to decide what this new age brings. Our answer will be determined largely by answering this question: Who, really, are we?

In loving memory of Dad. Thank you for everything, and rest in peace.

Liberty means responsibility. That is why
most men dread it.

—George Bernard Shaw

Acknowledgements

Without the support and endless patience of my wonderful girlfriend, Sarah, this book simply would not have been possible. Thank you for standing by me through all of our challenges and seeing the good in me.

Thank you also to my amazing mum and recently departed dad, Kathryn and Ron, who have been there for me throughout my forty years on this earth. They have been forever loyal and forever loving.

Thank you also to my brother, Chris; my sister, Lizzie; all of my extended family; and friends old and new for their continued support.

Let me also show my gratitude towards all of my YouTube subscribers. Thank you for watching my videos and for all of your contributions towards *The Imperfect Individual*. You make me feel like I'm achieving something worthwhile.

Thank you to Matt Connors for supplying his incredible astronomical photographs, and to Gary Beach for his beautiful artwork.

Finally, a big thank-you to everyone who has contributed to the crowdfunding campaign for this book. I massively value your support and love that you believe in what I'm doing! As promised, here is a mention for each of you:

Kathryn Coffey   Del Thomas
Ron Coffey   Paul Bennett

Jim Adams
David Harris
Michael Glover
Chris Coffey
Rob Jones

Samantha Aikman
Siobhan Gorst
Magpie
Susan Newman
Britt Rubin
Chris Rimmer
Richard Kelly
John Carroll

Introduction

Imagine a glowing red sun sitting on the distant horizon, and ponder this: Is the sun setting on a golden age for western society, ushering in a dark night that never ends? Or is it rising to reveal a dazzling new day for humanity? Are the colours drab and grey or luminous and brilliant? Do you feel a cold chill, or are you bathed in a gentle warm breeze?

I ask these questions because I want us to consider the pivotal point in the history of human civilisation in which we currently find ourselves. I want us to reflect as deeply as possible why we think we are where we are, what we think will happen next, and most important how we will use our immense value as individuals to influence that direction. I want us to ask ourselves this question: How much are we willing to take individual responsibility for healing our world?

I recently read a quote that resonated with me enormously. You may already be aware of it.

> Hard times create strong men
>
> Strong men create good times
>
> Good times create weak men
>
> Weak men create hard times[1]

---

[1] G. Michael Hopf, *Those Who Remain* (Create Space, 2016).

These pertinent and relevant words by author G. Michael Hopf beautifully represent the nature of human beings and the societies that they are able to create, develop, destroy, create, develop, and destroy.

My aim in this book is to hypothesise that we are in the latter part of this cycle, facing hard times and tyranny and requiring strong characters to navigate the path to better times and freedom. I want to find out if I am a strong or weak person, and I want to encourage you to ask the same question of yourself. I intend to discover whether we have indeed moved out of an era of unprecedented good times and whether trouble, darkness, and even harder times lie ahead if we do not implement massive positive change to the way we see ourselves and how we interact with our world. I want to determine what got us to where we are, how we can each take responsibility now for stopping the madness that is enveloping us and save ourselves, and what we can do as individuals to contribute to a society that is more enlightened, intuitive, and altruistic.

I also want to determine the answer to this incredibly important question: Has ideology won the battle over ideas? Have political and scientific creeds taken control of the lives of many, and has the well of individual philosophy and conceptualisation run dry? If so, what dangers does this pose, and what can we do to return to a world where ideas are encouraged and healthy debate is fundamental to all aspects of public life? What can we do to ensure the return of the inalienable freedoms granted to us as our birthright but so carelessly handed over to an all-consuming state?

It is illuminating that, at the age of forty, I am finally able to approach some level of understanding of myself and my place in the world, providing the inspiration to write this book. When I look back on my life, I see that it is defined primarily by three entities: suffering, curiosity, and evolving purpose. Based on my understanding so far, it is becoming clear to me that the unearthing of and pursuit of purpose is reliant on learning through suffering (which is an inevitability for all of us) and unbounded curiosity. The suffering provides context and learning, and curiosity give rise to ideas and values. It was only when I had the realisation that a life containing suffering was not only unavoidable but the actual catalyst for meaning that I began to understand myself on a deeper level. I had always wondered why I never really felt calm, why I was uncomfortable in so many environments, why so much in my world seemed to make no sense to me, and why I was confused and frustrated at the mass conformity to lifestyles and outlooks that I observed around me. I think that on some level, I was aware that I was allowing society to dictate my life for me, but despite my questioning mind, I didn't know how to be true to myself, how to be authentic.

I have had many jobs, including working as a paperboy, dishwasher, retail assistant, barman, waiter, tax administrator, accommodation officer and residential hall manager at a university, Facebook marketer, and delivery driver. I have travelled to twenty-one countries, lived in Spain, passed one degree and quit another, had six operations, nearly died once, and placed myself in terrible danger many times. I have met, interacted with, and been friends with people from many different backgrounds and countries. I have dealt with periods of deep and lasting depression and angst and experienced times of great joy. I have developed problems with alcohol and gambling. I have experienced great physical and mental pain. I have hurt those closest to me, shunned their kindness, and shown myself to be selfish and sometimes even feckless. I have felt the presence of demons and worked to slay them—a never-ending process. Throughout, despite the suffering, I have always had a curious mind, adding to my well of knowledge from each experience, event, or interaction. I have always been wary of ideology and tried to cultivate my own ideas.

I write this sentence in December 2021, the final month of the most difficult year of my life, a year in which I lost my beloved father. Yet this is also the year that I have truly felt guided by a higher power. The suffering has taken on a deep and insightful meaning. My purpose is slowly unfolding. I can feel it. I am expressing it through this very book. Just like a river, which meanders and ebbs and flows before pouring into the sea, so the same happens for our own direction in life. The journey is challenging and confusing, but one day, you will look back and see that it all made sense. Never stop being curious. Never stop asking questions. Never be cowed in your quest to discover yourself.

I wrote much of this book in 2019, exploring themes relating to individualism, society, purpose, identity, ideology, fear, and polarisation. It was my attempt to understand and critically analyse the rapidly changing societies and culture in the West, make sense of the individual's own place in it, and identify dangerous themes emerging that appeared to point towards an ebbing away of the sovereignty of the individual in favour of the state, the herd, and the group. I had long been interested in history, society, and personal development—reading books, watching documentaries, and undertaking self-help courses. Yet my main drive towards trying to understand myself, my place in the world, and why society appeared to be heading in a chaotic and dangerous direction came via regular introspection and simply watching people, particularly when they were interacting as part of a group. As the years crept by and my curiosity and fascination grew, I felt compelled to try to clarify my ideas in the form of a book. After all, if not me, then who?

However, the book lay incomplete—twenty thousand words on a laptop, nagging away at me, just another unfinished undertaking of many in my life. In the time between me starting my book and resuming my writing, humanity was suddenly confronted with a challenge, the likes of which hadn't been faced since the Second World War. The challenge came in the form of COVID-19 and the associated unparalleled societal response. I convinced myself that the threat combined with the upheaval was so stark, it would trigger a much-needed collective awakening across the world and that the madness, paranoia, derangement, and ignorance displayed by many individuals, reflected in the mainstream media, and vented on social media would largely disappear. I thought something kinder and more discerning would take its place and that nuance, complexity, and respect would return to public discourse. I told myself that the themes I tried to explore in the first draft of the book in 2019 were now irrelevant, redundant, and unrepresentative of these new, more emotionally mature times.

It seems that I was wrong. What I originally wanted to say has become even more relevant.

In this book, I will attempt to recognise, discuss, and give context to the issues that we all face in our confusing and fractured world. I will at times paint a bleak and pessimistic picture. I will be honest and forthright in attempting to explain our situation. It may make you feel uncomfortable at times as you realise that you are more than likely part of the problem, just as I am. However, I also want to give rise to hope within you and explain how we can all choose to be part of the solution—a solution that must be discovered before our world descends into a darkness from which it cannot escape. I will therefore attempt to provide answers to our myriad of problems and how we can all as individuals draw out the courage, authenticity, creativity, and understanding needed to heal our world and move us towards a brighter age. I want to do this by offering a glimpse into a happier future, one in which we can choose to live a life guided by values and purpose. As you shall see in this book, since unearthing and pursuing purpose in my life, I have embraced deep responsibility, understood my essential values, and lived more courageously and authentically. I know that I can and do make a huge, positive difference to a world desperately in need. The important relationships in my life have been fortified and grown into something even more beautiful, I have connected with and inspired many people through my YouTube videos, and I have been part of a resistance movement of local people with similar passions for protecting and defending basic human rights at a time when they have been and continue to be under siege.

My aim is not to pin blame or draw conclusions relating to who may be pulling the strings of society or what dark forces in the shadows may be controlling our destiny. I'm not going to examine the power and influence of major organisations, countries, or specific individuals or theorise or hypothesise about an imagined nightmarish future. I believe that many other writers and commentators are already doing this. Instead, I want to talk about people, both from an individual and societal angle. I want to show you what I have observed in my own country and try to stitch together a tapestry of where Western society is currently at based on my own insights. This book is less concerned with information and more with perception. It is, nevertheless, a critique on a Western society that, as I shall argue, has failed, and it provides context on what got us here and what we need to do now to tip the scales from centralised, top-down control and surveillance and towards true liberty and self-determination.

The Madness
Indoctrination and Psychosis

Dystopia is Here

I find it intriguing to wonder how historians will judge the last few years—that is, if they will even be permitted to tell the story. How will they attempt to make sense of a world that appears to have morphed into a dystopian farce far beyond what even George Orwell and Aldous Huxley imagined? I believe that history will judge this generation severely on how we handled and responded to the challenge presented to us in the early 2020s. I will expand on why I think this is so in these pages. But what about those of us mired right now in this bizarre and dangerous reality? What are we to make of it? How are we to understand a world that now appears to be so far detached from the key concepts that have always underpinned human existence—connection, community, conversation, purpose? And where will we ultimately end up? These tumultuous times may not be about to end any time soon and may likely worsen further, but in time, end they will. But then what?

Before I examine our recent and present times and try to explain them, let me offer a glimpse into the future that I believe will emerge once our current era of insanity, division, and chaos is over. Let me also acknowledge with hope in my heart that the seeds of intellectual, moral, and spiritual regeneration have already been sown, and tender green shoots are sprouting all around. I will talk more about this later.

A New Age of Conversation, Connection, and Community

I contend that, in time, a more altruistic, resilient, and emotionally mature society with new powers of perspective will emerge. We will live in the age of conversation, connection and community.

After decades of myopic, destructive, and moronic groupthink, people will rediscover the joy of creative, respectful conversation. The aggressive and regressive tribalism so commonplace right now will be replaced with complexity, richness, and balance. Respect will return to public life. We will once again realise that productive and fair societies are built on the gifts of individuals and that the cultivation of individuality is a societal value crucial to this. Meaningless, empty slogans, currently so fashionable and thoughtlessly embraced, will largely disappear as people insist on more cerebral, insightful, and philosophical debate. Freedom will be cherished. Lessons will have been learned about how liberty is precious, and people will be astonished and shocked at how they surrendered their freedoms so meekly in the face of aggressive media and government scare tactics. Education will be fundamentally different. Learning models and structures will nurture the imagination of children and students, focusing less on remembering and regurgitating and more on creating and inspiring. Celebrities will no longer be prominent in the public imagination as people realise that those celebrities stand for nothing but themselves. The mainstream media will be a thing of the past, and the BBCs, SKYs, and CNNs of the age in which we now live will be judged as agenda-obsessed spreaders of poison and propaganda rather than as vehicles for reporting news with fairness and balance. A new media, more balanced, representative, and driven by values centred around objectivity and truth, will emerge in its place. Social media will fade into oblivion as people realise its toxic effects on the individual and society and rediscover the joy of organic, face-to-face interaction. Health and safety practices will be massively scaled back as society recalibrates its attitude towards risk. Businesses and organisations will consider people's suitability for jobs based on character and skills rather than equality quotas, and workplace culture and productivity will be better as a result. Physical, psychological, and emotional health will be viewed in a wildly different manner than today, focussing more on introspection, nature, connection, and exercise. Pharmaceutical and tech cartels will lose their corrosive grip on power as people realise how toxic their influence on society had become. Governments will once again be scared of the people, rather than the other way round. Cancel culture will be viewed as immoral, immature, and deeply sinister—the ultimate example of a society that became very, very sick. Liberty will once again be the lifeblood of society, and self-autonomy will be the oxygen of altruistic individual and societal life. Freedom will be more important than safety. Diversity of thought and content of character will be more important than skin colour, sexual orientation, or gender. Fairness will be more important than equality. Self-analysis will be more important than self-identity. Individuality will be more important than group association. Authenticity will be more important than image.

Eventual evolution to a new age of conversation, connection, and community is inevitable as a natural and organic antidote to the deeply corrupt and mentally ill era in which we currently find ourselves. An intellectual and moral counter-revolution is already simmering and will eventually bubble to the surface in glorious form, sweeping away the tyranny, lies, and evil that presently preside over our world. Indeed, I have hope for the long term but also a sense of deep unease about our current situation and for what may lie ahead in the months and years to come. These questions are urgent: What has happened to our societies in the West, how can it be explained, and what can we as individuals do about it?

The Sanitisation of Life

A sanitised world looks something like this: It is one where a rapid revolution in language takes place, one in which words are categorised not according to what they actually mean but to what extent they may cause offence. Many of those words are excluded from public discourse and are replaced with hollow and meaningless expressions. Failure, instead of being viewed as a route to success and learning, is to be avoided at all cost. Mistakes are not tolerated and are punishable by loss of job and livelihood. A demented and sinister band of lemmings on Twitter, eerily reminiscent of a baying crowd at a medieval execution, gleefully call out those mistakes so the guilty individual can be publicly named and shamed. Those very same people attempt to cleanse the world of views they dislike, such is the level to which their own life has been sanitised. Image is more important than substance or character, and Facebook and Instagram are harnessed to create the illusion of perfection. Vacuous celebrities are omnipresent, exerting a degree of influence over millions of people completely out of tune with their lack of talent. Comedians churn out homogeneous, unimaginative material for fear of offending their politicised audiences. Musicians see themselves not as creators of epoch defining music but as messengers for the cultural establishment. Increasing numbers of people blindly subscribe to political ideology, absolving themselves of the responsibility to pursue nuance and strike balance. Individuals with different viewpoints are shunned and often vilified for fear of the internal conflict that may ensue at the possibility of having to examine and challenge existing beliefs. Safe spaces allow university students to be shielded from any views that may trigger their neurotic, flimsy characters. The population is bombarded with messaging telling them how they need to live their lives, ensuring they don't need to figure it out for themselves. Shoppers insist on purchasing fruits and vegetables genetically engineered to look perfect and presented in eye-catching plastic packaging. Schoolchildren compete in sports days where everyone receives a prize for taking part, and there are no winners or losers. The sport of football is subjected to regular micro reviews to ensure the rules of the game are being slavishly followed, removing the joy and spontaneity inherent since its creation. Repeated and organised attempts are made to overturn democratic outcomes. The mainstream media ceases to reflect public opinion and instead attempts to inform public opinion by incessantly lying and deceiving. Social media platforms ruthlessly censor content that doesn't tally with their ideological leanings. Imperfections are not tolerated, authenticity is in short supply, and insincerity, sanctimony, and sycophancy form the main narratives in society. People in their millions unquestioningly give away their hard-won freedoms and right to privacy in exchange for the feeling of safety.

What, then, would be the natural next step to this sanitisation of our world? What disturbing trend follows? Sanitisation from other people, of course.

A World of Zombies

The pitiful individuals in this nightmarish and paranoid society are told that there is a deadly disease in circulation. They are forbidden by the all-powerful state to leave their house except for a state-sanctioned bout of exercise lasting no more than one hour or to purchase essential items. They are not permitted to see their loved ones or to enter within a two-metre distance of any other person with whom they come into contact, save for people they live with. They must be careful not to breach any of these restrictions for fear of being reported by their neighbours and visited by the police, who may issue them with a fine. They must wear a cloth covering their face when out in public. They must obey strict instructions when shopping, robotically adhering to designated zones and keeping distance, all whilst ensuring they don't cough or sneeze for fear of being castigated by a terrified fellow shopper wearing a mask. They are indoctrinated with messaging on TV, radio, and the internet instructing them to avoid contact with other people at all costs. In their hordes, they religiously tune in to their TV sets at 17.00 every day for an hour-long update from the government about how their sacrifices of unquestioningly surrendering their freedoms to the state are key in defeating an invisible enemy. For twenty-four hours a day, they are subjected to relentless and intense propaganda from the mainstream media hammering home the message that this invisible enemy is killing hundreds every day and how they must obey without question the state instructions; otherwise, more people will die, and it will be their fault. The poor, terrified citizens are allowed one extra state-sanctioned trip out of their homes once a week but must ensure they go no farther than the end of their garden. This is to applaud, in unison, the National Health Service. From eerie silence, the air is suddenly filled with the sounds of metronomic clapping and banging of pans. After two minutes, the noise stops, and silence once again falls across the land.

The citizens of this era-defining event are brainwashed into believing that this is an invisible threat to their very existence. Their mantra of 'Stay Safe' is the ultimate expression of their society, which has become first preoccupied and then obsessed with all the wrong things. These poor, ignorant souls, who for years have been fed a diet of agenda-driven news with a strong undercurrent of threat, have lost their powers of resilience, their capacity to balance risk, and appallingly their appreciation of freedom. Their twenty-first-century need for safety and certainty is now in severe danger of being the very thing that destroys them. The deep state and media has softened them up for decades and, like a lion patiently watching its prey, goes in for the kill when they are at their most distracted and vulnerable.

Media and State-Induced Terror

I will always remember Saturday, 21 March, and Sunday, 22 March, as the weekend everything changed.

In the weeks prior, I was aware of what seemed to be a growing threat from a newly discovered disease called COVID-19, although most people seemed to be calling it coronavirus. At first, I dismissed the news around this virus as exaggeration and hyperbole. I had already become highly suspicious and sceptical of the mainstream media, and much of what I witnessed and read seemed to fit into the usual patterns: take a subject, imbue it with an ideology of fear, disseminate to the public, wait for the band of doom-obsessed social media foot soldiers to hammer home the message with sick delight, censor anything that strays from the 'accepted' version of events, and repeat ad infinitum. I had long before noticed how threats to our way of life regularly highlighted by journalists and their band of crusaders on Twitter never seemed to materialise. I wondered why they were constantly so obsessed with apocalyptic outcomes and seemed incapable of injecting any degree of positivity or balance into news coverage. But as time went along, slowly but surely my perception of this threat changed. I noticed how many normally level-headed people around me were now starting to worry. Amidst a growing concern, it became apparent that this was indeed a large-scale threat. The COVID-19 pandemic was going to kill a lot of people. It was going to rip through the population, causing mayhem and destruction. Hospitals would be overwhelmed, and no family would be spared its wrath. The fact that the government was talking directly to the people every day to provide updates was a sign that this disease was exceptionally serious. After decades of little to no real threat, this was our time to suffer.

By Saturday of that dreadful weekend, the fear was at its peak. The disease had begun to claim its victims, and projections indicated that it would soon be out of control. By now, many people were already deciding to stay indoors to protect themselves, many businesses were planning for closure, hordes were descending on shops to panic-buy items, and there was a palpable sense of real fear. I spoke to most of my friends and family at this time. They were all frightened. And now, so too was I. At work, I spoke to a customer, who told me she was a respiratory nurse in a local hospital. 'Is it really as bad as they are making out?' I asked her.

'Worse,' she said. 'Doctors are going to have to make heartbreaking decisions about who lives and who dies.' This chilled my blood. It was verification of what the news was saying. We really were about to be consumed by this killer virus. That night, my mood crashed and anxiety took over. I couldn't sleep, and when I did, I had nightmares where I couldn't breathe.

Virus, suffer, death.

Virus, suffer, death

Virus, suffer, death.

The message had hit home, as had my initial complacent and cynical approach to it. On Sunday, I developed symptoms. Oh, no! Was I to be one of the millions of victims? Had I passed this evil thing on to my family and loved ones? By this time, massive concern had taken over. My girlfriend, Sarah, was crying. I phoned work and told them I couldn't come in because I may have the virus. I was told that there was no requirement for me now anyway. The next day, the entire country went into lockdown. I was struggling to cope. I had no job, lost any sense of hope, and felt nothing but anguish and terror. I tried to numb the feeling by drinking heavily, and for the next few months, I sought solace in alcohol.

A Shift in Perspective

As the days slowly ground by, my perspective began to pivot once again. Something did not feel right. What was going on here? What could justify a comprehensive closing of most facets of society? On many levels, the mere idea of a lockdown of healthy people seemed to be beyond insane. Was this threat we all faced really as stark as we were being told? Were the measures put in place by the government and fanatically reinforced by the media in proportion to this threat? Why was there no discussion about the suffering that was beginning to take place across the country as people struggled to adapt to this new and claustrophobic way of life? I felt healthy—the cough and high temperature I had at the start of lockdown disappeared after one day—and not a single person in my circle had fallen ill. I found that strange. The situation started to feel a little too engineered, and the messaging from the media and government had become incessant and myopic. It felt like propaganda. Next came the videos of dancing doctors and nurses on TikTok. Surely if they were so busy treating patients, there would be no time for coordinated dance moves? This, in particular, was a clear red flag to me. And why weren't *they* social distancing? Then came the fanatical clapping for the National Health Service every Thursday. After participating myself for the first two weeks, I suddenly became very irritated. It felt too staged, too bizarre, too communist! Was this all a mass distraction from something else? Was this yet more propaganda?

As the days went, by I discovered that the British government had downgraded COVID-19 to a non-high-consequence infectious disease. This was done on 19

March—before lockdown had started! There it was in black and white on the government website. I then had a look at other official government documentation on the website from Scientific Advisory Group for Emergencies (SAGE),[2] who were informing decision-making. This made for a truly shocking read. Amongst many sinister paragraphs about how the public needed to be controlled in order to beat the virus, this one stood out as the most appalling: 'A substantial number of people still do not feel sufficiently personally threatened … The perceived level of personal threat needs to be increased amongst those who are complacent, using hard-hitting emotional messaging.' In effect, this was calling for a psychological war on the public. It was utterly abhorrent, disgusting, and malevolent. Had Joseph Goebbels written this? Yet chillingly, most people were unwilling to engage with the idea that there may be an alternative explanation to events, one far removed from that espoused by the media, or that the response to the virus had been grossly exaggerated, so consumed had they become by government indoctrination.

More evidence that we were not being faced with a disease deadly to the vast majority of people emerged. The death rate from the virus was exceptionally low, and certainly when taking into consideration the unbelievably strict measures that had been imposed in an effort to contain it. The vast majority of people dying were old and had existing illness. The virus was, quite clearly and demonstrably, not a threat to most people. Even the Grim Reaper himself—Chris Witty, Chief Medical Officer, advising the British government—said so. At the daily government press conferences, all of the evidence

---

[2] 'Options for Increasing Adherence to Social Distancing Measures', March 2020, https://assets.publishing.service.gov.uk/government/uploads/system/uploads/attachment_data/file/882722/25-options-for-increasing-adherence-to-social-distancing-measures-22032020.pdf.

showed the NHS coping well with the influx of patients. It became clear very early that they had overreached and overreacted. By mid-April, the disease was on the decline, yet the measures kept on coming, and the negativity from the media was increased even further. More and more voices were asserting that the response had been overplayed and tried to highlight the horrendous consequences on society due to lockdown—increases in suicide, child and domestic abuse, cancer referrals and treatments not taking place, hospital accident and emergency departments eerily quiet, old people dying alone in care homes, funerals taking place with no family members present, a mental health epidemic gripping the population, mass job losses. Yet these voices were rarely, if ever, heard on mainstream media. They didn't match the all-consuming narrative. What was this really all about, and how could any of it be justified?

As I write this sentence, our freedoms in the UK are still severely curtailed because we are in the midst of a third national lockdown. Most businesses are still closed. People are not allowed into the homes of any of their family or friends. Physical contact with anybody outside the immediate home is forbidden. Pubs and restaurants stand forlornly behind shutters. GPs, community clinics, and dentists are unable to see patients. Football stadiums, cinemas, and theatres are shut. Our country has been decimated, our economy destroyed, our society shattered. It will take decades to recover.

Before our eyes, a political, social, health, and economic revolution has taken place in the space of a couple of years, and many have not yet noticed. It is a revolution driven not by the people but by dark, malevolent forces. It is a revolution resulting not in the liberation of the population but the enslavement of them.

Brainwashing in Action

This revolution cannot have taken place without an expertly created programme of propaganda and the means to inflict it on an unsuspecting public. Watching this propaganda wrap its evil tentacles around society and convincing nearly all, including myself in its early stages, of its message has been chilling.

In attempting to understand the poisonous intentions behind mass propaganda, we must consider these infamous words, attributed to Joseph Goebbels, minister of propaganda for the Nazi party and chief architect of the narrative which convinced the German population to mass murder millions of people during the Holocaust: 'If you tell a lie big enough and keep repeating it, people will eventually come to believe it. The lie can be maintained only for such time as the State can shield the people from the political, economic and/or military consequences of the lie. It thus becomes vitally important for the State to use all of its powers to repress dissent, for the truth is the mortal enemy of the lie, and thus by extension, the truth is the greatest enemy of the state.'

In reflecting on my societal observations in the early 2020s it has become clear to me that the lie that has been told, and continues to be told, is of incredible, incomprehensible magnitude. It is a lie that has resulted in the biggest assault on human rights for centuries and led to the unnecessary death, injury, and suffering of untold numbers of people. Worse, it is a lie that has been swallowed by the majority. As I write, there are growing and welcome signs that a largely obedient, trusting, and naive public are finally beginning to ask questions, and thus the censorship of anything that deviates even slightly from the message that governments want to project is becoming established. Just as Joseph Goebbels told us, the truth indeed is the mortal enemy of the lie.

What Starts with the Burning of Books Ends with the Burning of Bodies

It is a strange and liberating phenomenon indeed to consider that the doorway to my own truth has been flung wide open during a time of external difficulty, oppression, and tyranny. This urgent compulsion to express how I perceive the world and my place within it has led me to write this book. And yet, as I exercise my fundamental and inalienable right to express my thoughts via my words, I have fallen prey to the censors of our age. Joseph Goebbels may be rotting in hell, but his putrid spirit lives on. Let me explain.

After I had written twenty-seven thousand words of the book, I began to research various publishing options. After careful consideration, I decided to opt for the traditional publishing route, so I sought a publishing agency that appeared to be a good fit for my values. After some time, I discovered a company that seemed right. I contacted them and had a very productive and friendly conversation. They were intrigued by my idea and were keen to work with me to bring my book to the world. They asked me to send my manuscript in its present, unfinished form so they could find out more and tailor their services towards my particular requirements. We discussed editing, cover design, price, marketing strategies—everything. A few days after sending my unfinished manuscript, I received this email:

Hi Dave

Thanks for sending this through. It reads
well and is coherent. Unfortunately, on
reflection, it's not something we'd be able
to publish in the current circumstances,
I'm sorry about that.

Regards

My instinct told me that the reason for their decision
was related to the COVID-19 situation. Nevertheless, I
immediately contacted them by phone to ask for some
more detail. I was unhappy that, after much time spent
researching options, choosing their services, and
extensively discussing the project with them, a brief
email had seemingly killed everything.

The person I spoke to was the same person who had sent
the email, who was the same I had previously spoken to
at length. This time, her attitude was completely different.
She was unfriendly, suspicious, unhelpful, and hesitant.
And she was pitiful in attempting to explain the decision.
I pressed her on why the idea of publishing my book
had been dismissed, and she repeated her line about
'the current circumstances'. I asked for more information,
and she garbled something about the need to keep
everyone safe and the NHS wards being full. Clearly, my
book had fallen foul of the truth police! I asked what on
earth this had to do with the decision to not publish my
book, and she was unable to answer, other than saying
it was somebody else's decision. I asked to speak to
this person to find out more information, but she told
me this wasn't possible. I asked her how she felt about
working for a censorious company and if she agreed with
me that at a time of rising tyranny, it is important that
books containing ideas that deviate from the narrative

are allowed in the public domain. She dismissed me and hung up the phone.

Do you know the most terrible thing about being censored? It's not the anger or the frustration or the confusion. It's the sense of helplessness. It's the realisation that what you have to say has been deemed unacceptable. It's the sickening feeling of knowing that your truth, expressed through your words, has been categorised as too inconvenient and so must be hidden from those who may wish to be exposed to it.

Similarly, a video for my YouTube channel (also called *The Imperfect Individual*) suffered the same fate. I use my channel to explore the themes that I discuss in this book, and in this particular video, I wanted to describe what I saw as moral vanity being expressed about the NHS via the mainstream media. I titled the video 'Are You Sick of Being Lectured to by Doctors, Scientists and Journalists?' I simply wanted to expose the unfair and unbalanced news reporting concerning the NHS as well as highlight that many of the people dispossessed and harmed due to the measures implemented by the government were not being represented at all by our media. I was dismayed when YouTube removed the video, citing that I had provided medical misinformation and had made people feel unsafe. To quote directly from the email I received:

> YouTube doesn't allow content that explicitly disputes the efficacy of local health authorities' or World Health Organization (WHO) guidance on social distancing and self-isolation that may lead people to act against that guidance. It is our job to make sure that YouTube is a safe place for all.

I appealed YouTube's decision and provided proof that I had not provided medical misinformation. In fact, I didn't even mention social distancing or self-isolation, let alone offer guidance contradictory to that of the World Health Organisation! I also asked why they were insinuating that my content could make people unsafe when I was merely expressing an opinion, and, I wondered who had the authority to judge on this. But it didn't matter. Their response was brief and served only to reinforce what had already been said. I have since had a further four videos from my channel removed by YouTube, simply for expressing an opinion. And therein lies the problem: at a time of rising tyranny, the quest for truth must be eliminated from the equation, for it is simply too much of a threat to the repugnant lie.

How Would You Respond
Given This Scenario?

Take a moment to imagine it is the end of 2019 again. You have been transported back in time and have within your power the ability to dictate what will happen to society in the next twelve months. The fate of the world rests on how you respond to the following scenario.

Next year, humanity will be visited by a virus. This virus will have an overall death rate of less than a quarter of 1 per cent[3] and an average age of death of eighty-three.[4] It will disproportionately affect old people who are already in poor health, but the vast majority of people infected will have only mild symptoms or no symptoms at all. In order to respond to the threat of this virus, here is what we are planning to do.

---

[3] As of 22 September 2021, a total of 158,664 deaths were registered in the UK with COVID-19 on the death certificate (https://coronavirus.data.gov.uk/details/deaths). It has been difficult to find a statistic as to what the death rate is or even what the definition of 'death rate' may be. We can use this statistic, divide by the total population of the United Kingdom, and multiply by 100 to arrive at a figure of 0.23 per cent, but this is most certainly artificially high for two reasons: (1) The timespan encompasses about eighteen months, so the statistic shows only cumulative deaths with a particular disease and nothing more (how many people have died of heart disease, cancers, etc., in the same period, for example, and are these figures higher or lower than usual?). (2) It is now known that a significant number of these deaths were in fact caused by other health conditions and that the presence of COVID-19 on the death certificate was on the basis of a positive test in the twenty-eight days preceding death.

[4] https://www.ons.gov.uk/aboutus/transparencyandgovernance/freedomofinformationfoi/averageageofthosewhohaddiedwithcovid19.

We will focus on tackling this virus at the expense of *everything* else. We will tell all people to stay in their homes, even if they are perfectly healthy. Hospitals will no longer carry out routine operations, GP surgeries will shut indefinitely, and other medical services such as dentistry will be withdrawn. Cancer screenings will be suspended, and many cancer treatments will be halted. Support services for drug addicts, alcoholics, and abuse victims will cease to be. Churches will turn away their parishioners. The economy will be utterly decimated as we will pay tens of billions of pounds to some people for doing nothing, and we plan to make millions of others jobless. We will create conditions whereby small businesses find it impossible to operate and so will have to shut. We will stop anyone from going to pubs, restaurants, football matches, and theatres. We will coerce everyone into forgoing contact with other human beings. We will spend one-sixth of the health budget on a testing regime, and we will persuade people to go for a test even though they are perfectly healthy. We will stop children going to school and will subject them to a constant drip feed of fear; when they do finally go back to school, we will stick cotton buds up their noses twice a week and require them to wear face coverings for six hours a day. We will create a campaign of indoctrination so powerful that people in their millions feel overwhelmed with panic and anxiety. We will remove old people from hospitals and send them to care homes. Many of these old people will die because we will remove their medical care, and the rest of them will be deprived of seeing their loved ones. We will make everybody wear masks when they go out in public. We will create mass messaging to ensure that everybody feels terrified all of the time, and we will reinforce this fear via twenty-four-hour media coverage, daily government press conferences, and mass advertising across TV, radio, and the internet. We will put up billions of signs across the land telling people to stay safe, not go near other people, and wear a mask. We will have police hotlines so people can report any rule-breakers. We will create new legislation so that if people want to protest against our measures, they will be arrested by police. We will collaborate with social media companies to ensure that anyone wanting to challenge our strategy is faced with censorship. We will finally come up with a cure to the problem in the form of an experimental and untested vaccine with serious safety concerns, and we will attempt to force as many people as possible to take this through means of state-sponsored blackmail and bribery. We will create a narrative so powerful that most people will forget that they still have their intuition and their immune system. We will completely re-engineer society.

Please, can you now advise us on whether we should go ahead with our plans?

If the decision was left to you, how would you answer? Would you see the proposed plan as sensible, just, humane, feasible, and in perspective? Or would you be shocked and horrified that these measures could even be conceived of in the first place and suggest something a little more in proportion to the threat? And yet the vast majority of people in my country and in countries across the globe have been willing acceptors of this new world, with all of its wickedness and backwardness. People in their millions have successfully been manipulated to such a degree that they have been totally disarmed of their capacity for critical thought and had their moral compasses recalibrated. They have allowed evil to happen right under their noses. Their souls have been darkened and their hearts have been blackened. They have been brainwashed. Horribly, many don't even realise it.

The lesson from all of this? When a lie is so huge and so monstrous, it is easier to compel one billion people to believe in it than just one person. Indeed, one of the enduring mysteries of human nature is that the more deranged and destructive the idea, the bigger the crowd that believes in it.

What Does Mass Embracing
of Masks Tell Us?

One of the greatest achievements of all by the propagandists was in their coercion of nearly every person to wear a facemask when out in public. In doing so, the masses, upon hearing the cry of 'do this for the greater good' dutifully sacrificed their individuality and, whether willingly or unwittingly, became a walking visible symbol of government oppression—just another tool in the weaponry of the propagandists used to maintain an ever-present level of fear.

When mandatory mask wearing was first introduced in July 2020 I entered into a state of abject shock, which had a deep and profound effect on me. I was horrified at the measure itself but even more so with the ease by which most people seemed to easily adapt to this new way of public life. How could so many people thoughtlessly embrace such a repressive idea without considering whether the measure actually worked? Indeed, for many months prior to the introduction of masks, the message from government and scientists had been that masks were not effective. Prior to July 2020, social media posts advocating for mask wearing to tackle the spread of COVID-19 were removed and labelled as disinformation. Moreover, how could so many embrace a practice that was backwards, undignified, and completely incongruent with Western society? How could so many accept this new normal without question? How could so many hide behind the ubiquitous slogan 'I'm keeping everyone safe' without explaining what that actually meant? How could so many fail to see the plethora of horrendous consequences associated with mass wearing of masks?

After my shock subsided, I became curious about this warped and weird behaviour. The same questions kept returning. Why hardly any resistance? Why no discussion? And the biggest question of all: What did this say about our society? I began to draw the conclusion that ubiquitous mask wearing by a sleepwalking population was an outwards manifestation of a number of serious and deep problems in Western society—a society that had lost its way, was lacking in vision, and most significantly did not understand itself. In many ways, the physical act of placing a mask over the face seemed to be the natural end point for a people who had been wearing a metaphorical mask for their whole lives. It was a visual demonstration of a society consumed by confusion, absence of purpose, and self-loathing.

Face to Face with Monsters

Sometimes something happens that is so shocking, you struggle to process the event. This happened to me on Christmas Eve 2020. It was the moment that I realised that my country was heading down a truly dangerous and terrifying path.

It was a cold and sunny day. I set off for my daily walk and filmed some content for my YouTube channel. I was looking forward to spending Christmas with my family. I felt good. Late in the morning, I visited a local pharmacy to collect a prescription. That was when it happened. That was when the malevolent, invisible force that I could feel wrapping around society presented itself physically to me in the form of two pharmacy assistants. Upon entering the shop, I was asked by the first assistant why I was not wearing a mask, to which I replied that I was exempt. She proceeded to ask why I was exempt, so I said it was none of her business. Already slightly aggrieved at this point, she then said to me that wearing a mask protected others from COVID-19 and that I should be wearing one. I explained that I had asthma and therefore was exempt. At this point, the other member of staff joined in, and together they continued their line of aggressive questioning and lecturing. I could feel the ire rise within me. I attempted to reason with the women and ask them to provide proof that masks worked in counteracting a virus, and if so, whether the positives associated with their use outweighed the litany of negative consequences for not only the individual wearing them but also society as a whole. I went on to explain again that the reason I was exempt was because I have asthma, but they replied saying I shouldn't be in the shop and should have my prescription delivered. They refused to listen, demonstrated zero empathy, and then ordered me to leave the shop for failing to comply. Of course, I refused, but that wasn't the point.

As I looked at these women, I realised that I was peering into the eyes of monsters. I was looking into the abyss, into the pit of despair. How many more of these state stooges were there? How many others were willing to bully, coerce, and denounce their fellow citizens for failing to comply with the rules? And the biggest question of all: what wicked acts, should the opportunity and circumstances present themselves, would these women and their ilk be capable of inflicting on others?

If you have even the merest appreciation of European history in the twentieth century, you will be able to guess the answer to this question. And it is because so many people seem to have little to no understanding of recent historical events, as well as the human condition in general, that we are at the cusp of a new age of totalitarianism. They do not realise that they too are at the mercy of the state machine with the capability of corrupting their minds and souls and turning them into demons.

One of the most impactful experiences I have had in my life was when I visited the Auschwitz Nazi concentration camp in Poland. On the tour, we were shown the harrowing proof of what happens when enough individuals surrender their thinking and their morals to the state—namely, death, mayhem, and cruelty on an unimaginable scale. I remember being particularly moved by the sight of masses of human hair, thousands of pairs of tiny shoes, and hordes of suitcases all housed behind huge panes of glass. I couldn't process the fact that the hair belonged to mothers, the suitcases to fathers, and the tiny shoes to young children, all of whom were robbed of their possessions and dignity before being sent to die in a gas chamber simply for not being born with the 'correct' genetic characteristics. But more than this, I wanted to understand how something so evil could occur on such an incomprehensible scale. How could so many millions of individuals be persuaded into being either complicit in this genocide or active and willing participants?

Primo Levi, an Italian chemist who survived his internment at Auschwitz, attempts to answer this question in his book *If This Is a Man*. Levi reminds us, with these cutting words, that state-sponsored tyranny and mass murder is simply impossible without the endorsement of millions of ordinary men and women: 'Monsters exist, but they are too few in number to be truly dangerous. More dangerous are the common men, the functionaries ready to believe and to act without asking questions.'[5] This raises the most difficult of concepts for every human being to grapple with, should they be sufficiently aware—that which implies that the potential for evil lies within each one of us. How else to explain humans' inhumanity to others throughout the eons of human existence? How else to explain the horrors of the twentieth century in Germany, Russia, China, Cambodia, and countless other countries? As Levi says, the problem is not that evil tyrants exist but that whole populations allow themselves to be consumed by their ideologies without challenging what they are told, simply because this is the easiest thing to do.

The evil residing inside each individual is not suddenly unleashed. Rather, it lies deep within the soul, waiting, menacing, ready to be brought slowly to the

---

[5] Primo Levi, *If This Is a Man* (Orion Press, 1947).

surface should the appropriate circumstances present themselves. The Nazis, spearheaded by Hitler and Goebbels, were terrifyingly proficient at drawing this evil to the surface in tens of millions of their compatriots. And how was it done? First, create a common enemy and a story around this enemy. In the case of the Nazis, the common enemy was the Jew. Next, force relentless and constant propaganda on the population, supporting the narrative that the enemy is an existential threat and that everyone who is not the enemy is of superior moral virtue. Finally, create the environment using changes in laws and legislation whereby the brainwashed individuals can carry out the bidding of the state, oblivious to the fact that they have allowed themselves to become state sponsored terrorists. The descent to moral depravity in Germany during the 1930s and 1940s was not sudden but rather steady and slow. And this is how it happened: make the masses believe what you want them to believe by disarming them of the ability to think critically; encourage them to conform to expected behaviours and beliefs through intimidation and coercion; watch as they begin to turn on the enemy as their souls become ever more corrupted; encourage them to persecute the enemy by robbing them of their possessions, destroying their businesses and removing their legal rights; and finally order them to commit mass murder.

It is alleged that Mark Twain said, 'History doesn't repeat itself, but it often rhymes.' Chillingly, in my own country, the rhyme has reverberated in a disturbing manner. I have observed a population that is largely unquestionably obedient, mostly devoid of the ability to challenge what authority is telling them, and lacking in the moral fibre to examine their conscience. They may be aware on some level of what horrific crimes happened in the name of ideology in the twentieth century, but they don't appear to understand it. The devil is stirring in their souls, and horrifyingly, they aren't paying attention. So the worst of them stop desperate people visiting dying relatives in hospital, isolate terrified and confused old people in care homes, stop children going to school and seeing their friends and family, refuse to treat sick patients, bully and intimidate, and force needles containing an experimental and deadly injection into the arms of unsuspecting people. And most of the rest say nothing and simply allow it to happen.

Psychosis and Persecution in the Name of the Common Good

How easy it has been for the propagandists to lull the citizens into psychosis, and how difficult it has been for those same citizens to free themselves. Once the spell of fear and suspicion has been cast, it is fiendishly difficult to break. Indian philosopher Jiddu Krishnamurti is said to have remarked, 'It is no measure of health to be well adjusted to a profoundly sick society.' How telling I have found this to be as I have witnessed people adapting and even thriving when the most ludicrous and immoral demands have been placed on them. It is worth remembering that even though the methods of instilling and manifesting large scale paranoia and insanity are different, the basic premise is the same, as has been witnessed throughout history during other times when societies have turned mad. We can look to the witch trials of the Middle Ages, the Spanish Inquisition, the Holocaust, the Marxist Russian revolution, Mao's cultural revolution, and the Killing Fields of Cambodia for other relatable examples of when populations have been manipulated into believing something monstrous; descended into the moral abyss; lost all power of reason, rationality, and logic; and become fixated on an idea so destructive that it leads to warped behaviour, deluded beliefs, and ultimately mass suffering and death.

And just as with all of the above examples, the total reordering of society and its values has been justified with the promise of protecting the common good. The enemy has this time not been suspected witches, heretics, Jews, the bourgeoisie, capitalists, landowners, political adversaries, or intellectuals. This time, the enemy has been twofold: first a virus, and second anybody who has wanted to open a discussion about the true deadliness of the virus as well as challenge the measures imposed by the government. The cry from the establishment has been the same as it has ever been: 'We will keep you safe.' As former US president Ronald Raegan famously said, the most terrifying words in the English language are, 'I'm from the government, and I'm here to help.'

These are just some of the measures that have been implemented in my country, all in the name of the common good: Mask wearing was enforced at blood donation sessions so even if you were exempt, you were excluded from donating blood. Official guidance from St John Ambulance was changed to require first responders not to perform mouth-to-mouth resuscitation on an unconscious person. Old people were isolated from their lifelong partners when they fell ill, and they died alone in care homes. Relatives of critically ill patients in hospital were forbidden from visiting them. Funerals were held in church car parks, and numbers allowed to attend were severely restricted. Whole year groups of children were sent home from school if just one child tested positive for COVID-19. Cancer referrals dropped by 60 per cent in April 2020,[6] compared to the same month in the previous year. The waiting list for treatment on the NHS rose to 5.5 million people,[7] which is the highest since records began and will likely be even higher by the time you read this sentence. Numerous small businesses folded. Suicides and mental health issues spiked due to the debilitating effects of lockdown. People were forced

---

[6] https://www.bmj.com/content/369/bmj.m2386.
[7] https://www.england.nhs.uk/statistics/wp-content/uploads/sites/2/2021/08/RTT-statistical-press-notice-Jun21-PDF-410K-69343.pdf.

to take experimental harmful injections so they could visit their families in foreign countries or stay in their jobs.

Who has made these decisions, and what right do they have to decide what is the common good? But again, as history shows, those who advocate for and then implement political philosophies that strive for the common good are absolutely the last people on earth any sane person would want in positions of power. With their delusional thinking, psychopathic tendencies, and insatiable lust for power, they are dangerous beyond words. Even worse are the lackeys, petty beaurocrats and underlings, who are always eager and ready to implement nonsensical measures and rules without question, blind to their own ignorance, bereft of morals, and devoid of emotional intelligence. With their endless Zoom meetings, fanatical mask wearing, worshipping of lockdown, adoration of rules, unhealthy appetite for issuing orders, and refusal or inability to observe the catastrophic impact their actions have had on society, these stooges, more than anyone else, have helped usher in a tyranny. Indeed, it takes only a few overlords to orchestrate and oversee a totalitarian regime but many ordinary citizens to accept, endorse, and implement it.

The Doctrine
Zealotry and Orthodoxy

Is the Spirit of Our Age a Lack of Spirit?

The experience of living in 2020s Britain shocks me anew every day, but it also presents a deep fascination. As I have watched a once highly liberal, free, and open society ripping itself apart, I have experienced a maelstrom of emotions. Some days I have felt a visceral anger, some days I have felt a debilitating sense of doom, and some days I have simply laughed at the incredible insanity on display everywhere I look. But I want to understand. Why has this happened, and how? Thus, I have spent many months pondering and trying to determine how a people can allow itself to be manipulated into behaving in ways antithetical not only to the values of a liberal and free society but also to the essence of what it is to exist as a human being. To fully comprehend my thinking, I had to wade deep into the psychology of this confused and pitiful society.

In summary, I believe that the country in which I live, together with many others in the West, is not only confused to the point of madness but also suffering from a paralysing lack of conviction and lacking in a worthy cause. On a subconscious level, meaning may be longed for, yet it is not understood how to find it. There is no altruistic aim, no common vision, no unifying truth. Thus, under conditions of rising oppression and relentless propaganda, this sense of captivating some common purpose begins to manifest in dangerous and deranged ways. Previous generations battled crippling poverty, fought wars against tyrants, and then built a society based on fairness, opportunity, and freedom. What about us? We convinced ourselves of the nobility in subjugation for the common good, lapped up the hero worship for standing two metres away from other people, patted ourselves on the back for muzzling ourselves in public, kidded ourselves that we were in a courageous and gallant war with nature, and proudly proclaimed on social media that we had been administered an injection. We stood in our little circles two metres apart, dutifully wore our masks, religiously sprayed hand sanitiser on our skin, and pretended that this unhinged dystopia of dehumanisation and robotic adherence to rules was to our benefit. And god forbid anybody who questioned this noxious doctrine or refused to participate.

We can go even deeper. Could it be that our age has become so distracted by triviality, so enslaved by ideology, so beholden to government and media, so chewed up by a lack of moral fibre and fortitude, and so devoid of meaning that a destructive and insidious societal self-loathing has developed? Are the people paralysed in a decades-long stupefying anaesthesia, waiting to rouse themselves and embrace sanity and morality once more, or could it be something darker? Just as the individual must destroy much of his character on the journey to truth, is the same now happening for Western civilisation? Must it implode before being born anew?

Why Did 6,103,056 People
Say No to Democracy?

As I staggered through my bleary-eyed, alcohol-soaked, depression-plagued days of my twenties and thirties, I slowly became aware of a society that didn't appear to be particularly healthy. I began to realise that the perception I had of not appearing to fit in wasn't due only to my own lack of direction, discipline, and purpose. Something was amiss with the world. There was something deeply wrong. There was too much politics. Politics was everywhere, all the time. As the years went by, I noticed the media narratives in my own country becoming more hysterical. Everyone seemed to be shouting about what was wrong, but nobody seemed to want to admit their part, let alone suggest a solution. The negativity was beginning to feel overwhelming. On 23 June 2016, an attempt was made to answer some of the questions and resolve some of the problems with the UK referendum on membership of the European Union. In the years that followed this vote, which the Leave side won 52 per cent to 48 per cent, it became clear that there was a deep, complex, and serious issue within British society and public life. Politicians, media, banks, institutions, big business, the EU itself, and even the supposedly independent speaker of the House of Commons repeatedly attempted to undermine a democratic vote by first delaying and blocking the UK's exit from the EU and then attempting to force a second referendum to ask the original question once again to a public they clearly thought had voted for the wrong outcome. This was astonishing in itself, but the most shocking aspect of all was still to come. On 20 February 2019, nearly three years after the Brexit vote, a petition was launched to Revoke Article 50. The intention was to ensure that the legal process whereby the UK could extricate itself from the EU was removed, thus ensuring the UK could not exit. Astonishingly, a total of 6,103,056 members of the public signed this petition. In doing so, 6,103,056 of my fellow compatriots declared themselves anti-democrats, openly stated that their vote was more important than those who had voted differently, and displayed their absence of maturity, perspective, and respect for democracy. This was the moment that I started to realise the depths to which my own country had sunk.

This coordinated movement to subvert democracy in the UK has not yet been processed and reflected on because the country has staggered from political chaos associated with Brexit to societal and economic chaos associated with the response to COVID-19. I therefore want to use this opportunity to provide a summary of the events leading up to and following the EU referendum in an attempt to shine a light on the disgraceful actions of all those who chose to vandalise the most important vote in the UK for forty years. This is not an argument for or against Brexit, nor an attempt to comment on whether it has been a success or not thus far. It is merely an effort to show the level of disdain for democracy that so many people in my country clearly possess. Together with the rest of the content in this book, I hope that it provides more context about the issues we currently face as a society. This book is not concerned with political matters, but please forgive my brief foray into politics as I try to paint a detailed case of just how deep the problem of anti-democracy appears to be in the UK.

In early 2015, David Cameron, then the Conservative prime minister of a government coalition with the Liberal Democrats, promised that in the event of the

Conservatives winning a majority in the forthcoming general election, he would hold a vote on UK membership of the European Union. British membership had long been afflicted with awkwardness and controversy since joining in 1975. Issues relating to immigration, identity, ethos, and economic and political viability had bubbled to the surface, resulting in louder and louder calls for the British people to have a say on membership. In the subsequent election, the Conservative Party won by a majority of twelve seats, so a referendum was arranged for 23 June 2016. In this election, the UK Independence Party, standing on an anti-EU platform, won 12.6 per cent of the total vote (an increase of 9.5 per cent on their performance in the previous election in 2010), a sure early sign of significant support in the population for leaving the EU.

As already noted, the referendum was duly held, and the Leave side won 52 per cent to 48 per cent (or by 1,269,501 votes). As discussed, the attempts to sabotage the outcome were set in motion, resulting in a febrile and unstable political atmosphere. The Conservative Party, by now led by Theresa May, attempted to strengthen its position and fend off the pro-EU rebellion by holding another election in an effort to increase their majority. This tactic failed and resulted in a hung parliament and even more instability. However, another clear message had been sent by the public as 84.2 per cent of votes were cast for parties committed to leaving the European Union—Conservatives, Labour, and UKIP. By late 2017, a more organised movement began to form centred around one idea: holding another referendum. It became clear that the UK's departure from the EU was turning into a battle of democracy versus despotism. As the shrill voices for Remain grew louder and the hopes of ever leaving began to fade, another important vote loomed on the horizon: the 2019 European elections. This was another opportunity for the British public to reaffirm their original position, and reaffirm it they did, rejecting the mainstream parties and voting for the Brexit Party, which had been formed specifically for the purpose of ensuring the UK left the EU. The Brexit party attracted 31.6 per cent of the votes. By this point, the anti-democrats had begun to point out that there was clearly an appetite from another section of the public to remain in the EU. They pointed to the large-scale protests in London and the fact that the Remain parties had also done exceptionally well in the European elections. What they failed to remember was that outcomes from four democratic events had provided clear instructions to the politicians that the British people wanted to leave the EU. What they failed to remember was that the referendum was organised on the back of an electoral promise and was endorsed by the majority of MPs. What they failed to remember was that referendums provide a snapshot of how a country views a situation at one particular moment in time. What they failed to remember was that democracy is sacrosanct and that there were no reasons whatsoever for it to be undermined. The protest movement arranged by the fanatical Remainers became more hysterical and intolerant. Indeed, the Liberal Democrats, who attracted significant support in the European elections, adopted a slogan of 'Bollocks to Brexit'. I remember at the time being aghast at this. How could a political party become so consumed by paranoia, insanity, and nihilism, and how could so many citizens allow themselves to be taken in by this? Bollocks to Brexit? Bollocks to democracy. Bollocks to respect. Bollocks to a different opinion. Bollocks to 17.4 million people. Bollocks to life.

Set against this feverish backdrop, a solution was desperately needed. The Conservative Party, knowing they absolutely had to enact Brexit to ensure its own survival, selected a new leader in Boris Johnson. He immediately began attempts to organise yet another election in order to win a healthy majority and make Brexit an inevitability. After yet more delays, blockages, and obstacles from an unhinged parliament, the vote went ahead on 12 December 2019, and the Conservatives won with a majority of eighty seats. Finally, nothing could stop it and Brexit could happen, which it did on 31 January 2020.

And yet many *still* can't accept the fact that the UK is no longer a part of the EU.

We Worship Strange Gods

What could explain this extremism, this zealotry, this dogma? Why, only two generations after hundreds of thousands of men and women paid the ultimate price in order to preserve the right to a free and democratic society in this country, did so many of my fellow countrymen and women decide to reject those principles and engage in democratic sabotage? Perhaps to find an answer, we can refer back to the quote at the start of this book: 'Hard times create strong men, strong men create good times, good times create weak men, weak men create hard times.' It appears our generation has made the fatal mistake that is seemingly ingrained in the human story—that of not learning from history. We are corrupted by complacency and convenience, are slaves to conformity and comfort, and have fallen into a deep coma. Life has become predictable, beige, bureaucratic, and overly structured, and we have allowed ourselves to become beholden to increasingly powerful government whilst being at the behest of an always rabid media. Our deep subconscious need for something meaningful to be part of, something bigger than us, has not been met in ways beneficial to the individual and to society because we have not allowed ourselves to create and imagine our way to this. We may have rejected God as we once imagined him to be, but we have reinvented him as a political ideology and institution. Welcome, therefore, to the church of the European Union.

And this isn't the only political God that we revere. The British National Health Service has, for many, taken on godlike status. Just as with the EU, the zealots instruct that we must worship at the altar of the NHS, genuflect to our saviours who work within it, and never, under any circumstances, commit the heresy of criticism. If this sin is committed, crucifixion awaits. The deification of the NHS reached its peak in spring 2020 when millions of indoctrinated followers took to the streets to clap in recognition of its righteousness and purity. Followers of Jesus bowed down to the cross. We clapped for our doctors and nurses. One of those followers was me. I'm not sure I'll ever fully understand the madness that possessed me for those strange few weeks. On the day I write this sentence, it has been announced that the NHS has been awarded the George Cross. This honour is awarded for 'acts of the greatest heroism or of the most courage in circumstances of extreme danger'. I have a huge issue with this, in that not only have I not observed acts of heroism and courage from staff within the NHS, but also I do not believe they were facing a situation of extreme danger. Indeed, I would suggest that the NHS, far from doing its supposed job of protecting the public, has largely done the opposite and committed great harm. But then, I forget that in this inverted world, the NHS isn't there to protect the public, but the public must protect the NHS. It is, after all, our God and must unflinchingly be served.

Our twenty-first-century gods are multiple and omnipresent and demand unquestioning loyalty and adherence to their doctrines. We see footballers taking the knee in an act of servitude, desperate to demonstrate to the world that they are eager to rid themselves of the shame associated with the sins of their ancestors. This is the Black Lives Matter god, which requires all white people to confess for the sin of being white and regularly check their white privilege. We see rainbow flags everywhere, emblazoned on face masks, hanging from windows, splattered across company website banners, and woven into footballer's bootlaces. This is the LGBTQ+ god, which requires all straight people to acknowledge the innate virtue in not being straight and the ongoing and constant oppression that all in the LGBTQ+ community face every day of their lives. We see large groups of middle-class snobs with plummy accents dressing in white, chaining themselves together, and telling us that we are destroying our planet and must be punished. This is the Extinction Rebellion god, which seeks to remind us of how abominable and abhorrent we are simply for being human, and will punish us all for this by removing as many freedoms as possible.

Our modern-day gods demand utter adherence to their creeds with even an iota of difference being looked on as the work of the devil. They expect total compliance and alignment with their message, and failure will result in denouncement, ridicule, ostracisation, vitriol and destruction. There is no forgiveness. There is no redemption. There is no salvation. There is no humility. There is no hope.

Science or Religion? Science is Religion

> God is dead. God remains dead. And we have killed him. How shall we comfort ourselves, the murderers of all murderers? What was holiest and mightiest of all that the world has yet owned has bled to death under our knives: who will wipe this blood off us? What water is there for us to clean ourselves? What festivals of atonement, what sacred games shall we have to invent? Is not the greatness of this deed too great for us? Must we ourselves not become gods simply to appear worthy of it?[8]

These prescient words from Friedrich Nietzsche served as a warning for the bloodshed and terror that was to tear apart Europe in the twentieth century, as well as the technocratic woketopia that currently has the West in its grip. The demise of religion, argued Nietzsche, surely left an existential chasm in the life of the individual and society. If God was indeed dead, then who or what would be the higher power? Who or what would be the truth and the light? Could humanity reimagine itself in sacred form and create a world of peace and abundance? Nietzsche was certain that this was not possible. As it turned out, the new supreme beings were Lenin, Stalin, Hitler, Mao, Pol Pot, Chaves, Idi Amin, and Castro. The Bible may have been cast aside, but the puppet master from beyond the grave, Karl Marx, already had the perfect replacement. The doctrine was communism, and the

---

[8] Friedrich Nietzsche, *The Gay Science* (Knopf Doubleday, 1882).

story that followed was one of famine, torture, misery, war, and genocide. We have been warned, and yet once again, we are allowing ourselves to fall prey to those who wish to destroy.

Societies today may no longer be so enslaved by bullets, but they are by information, statism, and utter absurdity. The physical threat may have diminished to an extent, but our brains and bodies are under siege. The tyrants may be in different form, but are the same in evil intent. Our existential question has become a crisis of the heart and of the soul. And we are insane. We have adopted science as our God. Science has become our religion, our guiding force, and our moral compass. What would Nietzsche have made of our world today, and could he have conceived of just how demented the masses became? What were they doing dousing themselves in litres of hand sanitiser, locking their children up at home, standing in pouring rain to have a cotton bud stuck up their nose to test for a disease even though they were perfectly healthy, agreeing to obscure their face with a rag every time they went out in public, willingly allowing themselves to be injected with an unknown substance and obeying orders of the most tyrannical and intrusive nature? And why, in doing all of this, did they explain it away by saying, 'I'm following the science'? What insanity! What heartbreak!

A Life of Regurgitation

A stable society built on solid foundational values and embracing qualities such as fairness, open-mindedness, debate, and community must be on guard against lurching to totalitarianism. Why, then, do we have a world with an ever increasing level of centralised totalitarian control and narcissistic elements embedded within? What has tipped the scales so decisively away from the sovereignty and respect for the individual and toward collectivism? Many have allowed themselves to be manipulated to such an extent, to become so hypnotised by government and media, and to become so devoid of critical thinking capacity that they have completely ceased to inform their own direction, cultivate their own ideas, and live by their own philosophies. Instead, they regurgitate what they have been told.

Life for the majority has become about living according to an accepted and staid template. Think of it this way. A child goes to school to be educated for a number of years in order to pass exams in which they are required primarily to regurgitate their rote learning. At school, they are discouraged from developing their own ideas because this doesn't fit with the established education model. They are expected to conform, obey, and hold their teachers in the highest possible esteem, for they know best. The child is then expected to go to university to continue his or her education so they can gain a degree and therefore have value to society. Their university education is once again based primarily around learning via repetition and then regurgitating information on exam day or repeating other people's ideas in dissertations and essays. At university, they are subject to an environment not based around the free exchange of ideas and robust and healthy debate but narrow-minded dogma. The student leaves university with a world view narrower than when they first entered and regurgitates what they have been told without question. The student attends a job interview, whereby they then regurgitate information they know the interviewer wants to hear, regardless of whether or not they believe in it. Depending on how rigidly they stick to the interviewer's agenda, particularly with issues relating to equality and diversity, they will be offered the job. The student is now an employee and will attend frequent and mostly pointless meetings, where they will regurgitate mostly inane and meaningless catchphrases and sound bites designed to impress, fill time, and distract from the task of achieving anything notable. The employee must attend training about how to think correctly and how not to be a racist, sexist bigot. If they correctly regurgitate the correct answers, they will be allowed to stay in their job, for they will have proved that they are not a racist, sexist bigot. The employee will now be in their late twenties, so now it's time for them to do some more regurgitating. They get married, have children, and buy a new car every two years. After all, that's the done thing, and that's what society approves of. Meanwhile, social media calls. There's no point in creating when they can so easily regurgitate, so they reiterate information that they agree with, mindlessly sharing posts with everyone in their own chamber of echoes. Vote Labour! Love the EU! Trump is a racist! Stay home and save lives! I love the NHS! I've had my COVID vaccine!

Regurgitate. Regurgitate. regurgitate. But here's the problem: In regurgitating so much, they have placed us all in danger. In the process, they have vomited bile over the memories of those who gave their lives for us and, even worse, the prospects of their own children.

The Age of Slogans

I mentioned earlier about my hopes for a new age of conversation to emerge from the shadows of these dark times in which we now live. Right now, we are still so far away from an age of conversation that it is sometimes difficult to even conceive of that bright, new age arriving. Instead, we live in an epoch where slogans and cliches have largely replaced conversation and ideas, and many individuals are too distracted, lazy, or ignorant to look beyond the empty words.

Hands, Face, Space. Control the Virus. Stay Safe. Get Brexit Done. Make America Great Again. Bollocks to Brexit. White Privilege. Black Lives Matter. Me Too. Build Back Better. Stronger Together. Slogans and mantras have become omnipresent in our world, present in advertisements and as expressions to summarise important projects and initiatives, as well as to programme the public into believing powerful narratives that have already been decided for us. They have largely replaced nuanced debate and have been employed to further infantilise an already infantilised public. It is essential that we look beyond slogans and explore subjects on a deeper level. We must reject the inane message behind these empty words and derive our own understanding of the situations and problems of our times.

Children as Propaganda Tools

Sadly, enlightenment, curiosity, and an urge to explore and discover are traits sorely lacking in today's woeful political, cultural, media, academic, and scientific establishments, reflecting society generally. Their insular outlook has narrowed to such a degree that they are increasingly incapable of making a convincing case for their often malevolent aims. Their relentless urge to grab or maintain power and control the overriding narrative around a subject is imperative, so they turn to children to do it for them.

During the height of the COVID-19 panic, I was sent a video which chilled my blood. In it, a series of Scottish children were filmed thanking their 'leader', Nicola Sturgeon, for keeping them healthy and safe. In the thirty-four-second video, a series of children say, 'The children of Scotland would like to say thank you to Nicola, our First Minister of Scotland. We are so grateful. Thank you for always keeping us safe, working so hard and for being strong for us. Thank you for caring for every individual life and for always thinking about the children of Scotland. Thank you Nicola. Thank you. Thank you. Thank you. Thank you.' In a similar way, in the early days of the COVID-19 pandemic, children were weaponised by the government and media into carrying out their propaganda for them. Suddenly the NHS rainbow, drawn by children and allegedly symbolising togetherness, hope, and unity, appeared in windows across the country. It was absolutely everywhere. It soon became apparent that there was little to no togetherness, hope, or unity in a country and society that is now beginning to realise that it has been subjected to a wicked campaign of lies and deception.

Perhaps the best example of a child being used as a propaganda tool is Greta Thunberg, the Swedish teenager who has acted as the establishment's spearhead in their fight against climate change. Her now infamous 'How dare you!' speech to the United Nations in September 2019 revealed a highly vulnerable and panic-stricken young girl driven by fear, paranoia, and climate doctrine. This autistic girl serves as the ultimate example of how children can be manipulated and used to plant the seeds of terror, alarmism, and paranoia in the minds of other children.

I am horrified at the way children in my country have been treated in the last two years. They have been ruthlessly terrorised, weaponised, and abandoned. If nothing else points towards a society badly in need of a candid conversation about its morality, surely it is ours and how it has treated its children.

Stay in Your Bubble

One of the most striking aspects of the last couple of years is how concepts that have been features of a society in rapid decline have manifested into actual behaviours. I admit to indulging in a little mischievous humour whilst observing this curious phenomenon because to most, it appears the symbolism is lost. I have previously talked about how the wearing of an actual physical mask on the face is the natural next step for a society that has worn a metaphorical mask for decades. Similarly, a generation who have overseen a society sanitised to oblivion now frantically and obsessively sanitise their own bodies with hand sanitiser. Another one of these intriguing concepts is that of 'bubbles'. Before March 2020, the idea that people must separate into groups called bubbles and not 'break the bubble' by associating with anybody not a part of their own bubble would have been dismissed as laughable and ludicrous. It *is* laughable and ludicrous. But in so many ways, the precedent had actually already been set. Society has been existing in a perceptual bubble for so long that the majority, when told to form bubbles and stay in them, complied.

There are a number of different themes in this book which attempt to explain and give context to why society has become so sick, but the one that underpins all of them relates to perception. We are currently existing in an era whereby perception has been manipulated to such an extreme degree that the most atrocious and immoral behaviours have become normalised and encouraged, and the most fundamentally basic human behaviours such as socialising, hugging, and breathing fresh air have been demonised. This has been achieved over a long period of time through a combination of schooling, media, social media, the film industry, advertising, and mass entertainment. It is difficult to conceive of anything more frustrating than asking somebody to consider that the version of events recounted by government and mainstream media might not be the full truth and then being dismissed, laughed at, or shouted down. Many have been placed in a perceptual prison by information, but finding the key to unlock the door so their minds become free once more has proven impossible in many cases. Perhaps the minds of these people never were free?

The System
Media and Control

Create Fear to Force Control

As with the earlier example of the Nazis, throughout history, the media and mass messaging has been used by governments to instil fear into populations. Worse, it has been used to create a narrative, which in turn becomes an accepted truth. Once a society reaches this point, the descent into horror can begin. This is playing out right now with the poisonous and malignant spread of terrifying propaganda and its corrosive effect on the moral outlook of many in society, as I have pointed out.

The mass media of the twenty-first century has morphed into a monstrous behemoth, promoting never-ending terror and incessantly repeating stories that aim to cause anger and fear. This is undertaken via an ever-present and never-ending sense of threats, very few of which manifest into something tangible and actually threaten people. As an example, the BBC news website on the day I write this features forty-one stories. Of these, twenty have a definite negative angle, and seventeen are neutral. This leaves room for only four stories which have an upbeat message. The words that jump out in headlines scream negativity, panic, and fright: Emergency! Disaster! Lie! Breaking point! Cancel! Racist! Big problem! Terror! Woes! Catastrophe! Warning! Dies! War! Condemn! Overwhelmed! Urgent! Horror! Crisis! The same pattern repeats in virtually all media: screaming headlines designed to instil fear and words aimed at evoking negative emotions. In the face of this, it comes as no surprise to me that people live their lives in an omnipresent state of anxiety. What's happening here, and across all of the other mass media outlets, is a calculated strategy of manipulation and control via the dissemination of information. The information used is very carefully selected for maximum impact. Whilst recent coverage has focused almost exclusively on the danger to people's health, very often the negative news stories are connected to the economy and to the climate. Those in power realise that the economy is an important factor in people's lives, so if they report alarming stories about a failing economic system, individuals will be even more fearful of making changes to their situations. I anticipate that as the narrative finally moves away from COVID-19, the media will pivot their news angle and attempt to cause mass anxiety about a failed economy and its disastrous impacts on people's lives. Even more than this, they will begin to paint a picture of an imminent climate change Armageddon. There are also other possible angles relating to Chinese and Russian aggression and expansionism that they may well pursue. Will it be a case of once bitten, twice shy, or are the masses ready to believe ludicrous narratives and fall for wicked lies once more? Please remember that when you watch the news, there is a cynical agenda being driven. That agenda wants to keep you scared, in line, and submissive. Instead, stay away from the mass media and consider consuming your information via smaller, less ideologically motivated agencies and individuals. In this way, you stand a greater chance of discerning something closer to the truth. I would encourage you to be vigilant in your consumption of the media and to start paying attention to the words used and the stories pushed. Are they positive or negative? Is there an unnecessary angle of fear to the story? Could they be twisting reality? Could they be lying to you?

Our ubiquitous mainstream media outlets are playing a destructive role in controlling how many people perceive their world and how they discern and process risk. For this reason, it is imperative to be independently minded, curious, and constantly open to changing your position on all topics. It is also absolutely crucial to subject yourself to opinion with which you tend to disagree. Only in being open-minded to the information via the media with which we choose to engage can we stand a chance of reaching a conclusion that hasn't already been decided for us. In doing so, we are far less prone to becoming indoctrinated. Most importantly, remember that your intuition is powerful and is likely pointing you towards truth. Use it! I will discuss intuition in greater detail later in the book because I believe the solution to the present confusion, inertia, and turmoil in the Western world lies in as many people as possible learning to embrace intuitive, heart-centred knowing.

Manipulation, Lies, and Hypocrisy

Even set against a landscape of hysteria and madness, there have been instances in the last two years where I have been shocked at how this once great country of mine has sunk to depths of incomprehensible fanaticism, and how the media has both displayed and orchestrated this deranged behaviour. One of those instances occurred on 25 May 2020. It said everything about how sick our mainstream media, and also our society, had become.

Dominic Cummings, who at the time was a senior advisor to Prime Minister Boris Johnson, had for the previous week been subject to a relentless media outcry regarding his alleged breaking of lockdown rules that he himself had helped implement. Incessant media led pressure was being applied on Boris Johnson to fire Cummings for this breach of lockdown code, and the pressure increased as each day went by until it became intolerable. The media were baying for blood, and eventually their demands were met. A press conference was hastily arranged in the rose garden at Downing Street, whereupon Cummings was subjected to a forensic interrogation live on television. It was unlike anything I have ever witnessed. His 'lockdown breaching' journey to north-east England was analysed in the most incredible detail, and he was battered relentlessly with a barrage of questions by journalists purporting to be acting in the national interest. Cummings was forced to read out a statement to the British people explaining in great detail the motivations for his journey, as well as a step-by-step description of precisely what he was doing and why at each stage.

The sickening glee with which the 'journalists' set upon Cummings was there to see for all who cared to look. They may as well have hung, drawn, and quartered him. Indeed, had they been given the chance, I'm sure they would have. There was one moment in particular that drew my attention and alerted me to the rabid intentions of the media representatives present. A journalist called Robert Peston strode arrogantly up to the microphone, asked Cummings a question which put him on the back foot, and then looked back to his colleagues with a look of sick delight. He then winked at them. Gotcha! His demonic look told me everything I needed to know. Our media were not seeking truth, were not looking to report objectively, and were not acting in the interests of the British people. They had an agenda, and they wanted to inflict this agenda on the public. And what was this agenda? To distract from something much, much bigger, as I shall explain.

In the weeks preceding the interrogation, the media had indoctrinated the British public regarding COVID-19. There was the fear-laden build-up as the disease began to get a foothold in the UK, followed by rolling news coverage of the havoc it was causing, encompassing ever-increasing daily death figures, and images from hospitals showing a health service allegedly on the verge of collapse. The aim, as I have already explained, was to frighten the British public into submission in order to buy their compliance and obedience. However, in the week of the Dominic Cummings saga, the disease had reached its peak and was beginning to lose its grip. Daily death figures were reducing rapidly, and fewer people were being admitted to hospital. I remember thinking that, if not cause for celebration, surely this was a reason for positivity and optimism. Surely the media, having dedicated close to 100 per cent of its coverage to the damage being wrought by the disease, would now apply some balance and report on the improving picture. Surely the media had a responsibility to help lift the mood of the nation and build confidence. But no. The only thing that mattered was one man's possible (probable) breaking of lockdown rules. Why? To distract, of course, which brings me to the next important point.

The ease with which the mainstream media was able to divert the public's attention away from the alleged ravages of the virus and towards the alleged misbehaviour of a government minister was astonishing. A public, who had until this point been wholly preoccupied with the threat (real or imagined) of a virus, had seemingly forgotten how scared they were and instead were revelling in joining with the moral condemnation of a public figure. I remember remarking to people that he wasn't alone in breaking lockdown rules. Indeed, many people, even at this early stage, were doing the same when it suited them. But logic had disappeared, along with perspective. Cummings had broken his own rules, had been found guilty via trial by media, and should pay the price. The media fanned the flames of indignation, people forgot they were supposed to be frightened to death of a virus, and I watched on, aghast. It was at this point that I realised the public had been deeply hypnotised by the media. Their minds were not their own. Like puppets on a string, they were dancing to the media's tune.

Can You See through the Media's Agenda?

I find it incredible that many are mesmerised to such a degree that even now, they cannot see the media's agenda. Every day brings a new example of manipulation, lies, exaggeration, hypocrisy, and unbelievable double standards. Two of the most vociferous individuals in their condemnation of Cummings were Sky News journalists Kay Burley and Beth Rigby. Their fake moral vanity in pretending to be true advocates of lockdown could barely be disguised by their venomous, bile-spewing rhetoric in connection to his alleged lockdown breach. A few weeks later, it was revealed that they too had broken lockdown, thereby rendering their previous feral commentary around Cummings hypocritical to the extreme. It didn't surprise me, though. These journalists, like most in the British mainstream media, weren't really contemptuous for Cummings or even for his alleged breaking of the rules. No, their contempt was for objectivity, for integrity, for humility, for truth, and for their own country.

As it turned out, 2020 was the year that the mainstream media in the West played their hand for all to see. It was the year that they abandoned all pretence of anything remotely approaching truth and instead made clear that their aim was to inflame tensions, create division, distract, whip up fear, and lie on a monumental scale. Their presence was all-consuming, and their narrative was dripping with poison. By June of that year, I was in a state of utter disbelief that the masses still couldn't ascertain what was going on, so blatantly rabid were the mistruths and so relentless the propaganda. During the first lockdown, which was largely adhered to by the vast majority at the start and then slowly unravelled as compliance began to slip and people began to leave their houses, I was working as a pizza delivery driver. Occasionally I tuned in to BBC Radio 5 Live, partly as my morbid curiosity got the better of me (how can their lies be *this* big?) and partly out of a genuine interest in hearing what I now deemed as my enemy was saying. There were many instances of coverage that left me shaking my head and screaming expletives to myself in my car, but one stood out. The summer had arrived, and people, understandably claustrophobic from months of lockdown, had escaped to the beach. The BBC was incensed by this. Colin Murray, presenter for the afternoon show, described these individuals as 'deadheads', saying that they were selfishly endangering the lives of others in creating a breeding ground for COVID-19 by breaking lockdown rules, forming large groups, and not observing social distancing rules properly. So much for the BBC adhering to its mission, namely 'to act in the public interest, serving all audiences through the provision of impartial, high quality and distinctive output and services which inform, educate and entertain'. This was just one example of the BBC, in clear opposition to its own mission, ostracising many of its former audiences (I know I'm not alone in being appalled at the BBC's descent into a state propaganda machine), showing clear bias (what could be more opinionated than calling a group of people 'deadheads'?), pushing low-quality content (where was the evidence for Murray's disdainful and disgraceful diatribe?), and acting indistinctively from its competitors (the rest of the mainstream print and TV media was also largely pushing the same narrative).

A few days later, Black Lives Matter activists were on the streets of London, protesting about the murder of George Floyd by a policeman in America. At this time, there were severe restrictions on the right to protest, and the media had already made clear their disgust for people protesting about the lockdown and associated taking of freedoms. These people, in the eyes of the media, were 'superspreaders', selfishly ignoring the health of others and idiotically breaking rules that were in place for the common good. Staggeringly, these criticisms did not extend to the people protesting in the name of BLM, even though the numbers were far greater and the protestors, it could quite easily be argued, were more animated and even criminal. But no, protests calling for racial equality and an end to white supremacy were seemingly exempt from lockdown rules and immune from media criticism. Why? Similarly, Donald Trump supporters attending his pre-election rallies were attacked and vilified for the same thing: selfishly congregating together in large numbers and risking causing a resurgence in the virus. A few weeks later, after Joe Biden's election victory, Democrats and their supporters were shown on TV hugging, dancing, and partying in large numbers. Was there any comment from the media about this? What do you think? I could elaborate further on this subject and provide many more examples of the media applying different rules to different groups depending on how they view the group's ideological and political position. In essence, group position in an imaginary hierarchy based solely on group identity dictates what standards the media expects the group to adhere to. There is more on this later in the book.

You will recall the character Dominic Cummings from earlier and how he was hounded mercilessly by the media for an alleged lockdown breach. Around a year later, Cummings—now out of government—appeared in front of a select committee set up to consider evidence that Cummings had submitted with regard to the British government's handling of the COVID-19 crisis. Amongst other allegations, Cummings appeared to be suggesting that lockdowns, so beloved by the media, had been resisted to a large extent by Prime Minister Boris Johnson and that he had implored Johnson to lockdown earlier and harder. Suddenly, the man who was public enemy number one for journalists was now being taken seriously. 'We must listen carefully to Dominic Cummings,' they said. 'We must find out what was said at those government meetings because the British people need to know.' I watched with scepticism and only a vague interest, seeing nothing more than a pathetic and ultimately meaningless Westminster pantomime. But crucially, a narrative was once again being spun by the media. Cummings, not long ago vilified, was now being taken seriously by the BBC, SKY, and the like. Why? Because what he was saying and the position he was taking now matched their own. As Shakespeare remarked, 'All the world's a stage and all the men and women merely players.' But here's the real question: What is the script? And, more importantly, who is holding the pen?

Break Free from Society's Trap

Taking into account the power of the media, it is little surprise that most people become highly conditioned followers cowed into accepting the status quo and their place within it, rather than leaders, creators, or innovators. From the moment we are born into this world, society surreptitiously begins to wrap its threads of conformity around us. The mainstream media and education system are key in enabling this to occur. Years later, the threads have morphed into a thick rope, tying us to perceived norms, behaviours, and outlooks. This is the perceptual prison. It is at this point that a person's true character has, to a large degree, been hijacked, unable to properly reveal itself. It is also at this point that the individual in question has become highly vulnerable to manipulation by those in power, usually via the media or social media. The individual has become oblivious to much outside of the mainstream narrative and is at risk of joining the indoctrinated herd. Few realise that this has happened to them. Those who do begin the confusing, painful, and arduous process of removing the ropes of conformity and obedience, thread by excruciating thread. The others remain ignorant, forever destined to remain roped to a set of expectations and rules, largely living their life as prescribed by society.

As well as the mass media and state education system, there is another prominent way that a society aims to control its citizens: distraction. Are you paying attention?

Give Them Bread and Circuses!

The ability to choose is one of the most fundamental rights a citizen possesses in a free society. We will all make good choices and bad choices, but for the most part, we are aware before we make the choice whether it will serve us well in terms of our mental and physical health. The issue for many lies in the propensity to sacrifice long-term evolution and development for short-term pleasure or diversion. And when it comes to short-term pleasure and diversion, we are ruthlessly preyed upon by predatory corporate powers.

The free market economy in the last forty years has morphed into an empire of cartels, resulting in an ever-increasing market share being taken by multi-billion-pound international companies, often at the expense of smaller, local business. The lockdowns since spring 2020 have only accelerated this trend. All of these huge corporate giants are expert at tapping into human psychology and adapting and sculpting their customers' behaviour and beliefs. Big business is becoming more expert at keeping us stupid, sedated, and sedentary so we will continue to buy their products without ever really asking why we need them. These distractions are all around and are always available for us as we demand ever more comfort, convenience, and pleasure—think of Facebook, Netflix, smartphones, Alexa, alcohol, gambling, junk food, and pornography as just a few examples. We can access these products with the swipe of a card or the click of a button, and all of them are bad for our health. Consider for a moment how easily controlled many are by these big corporations and how they exist to mould us into the laziest and most slovenly version of ourselves. We become ever more enslaved to the puppet masters of the technology, junk food, pharmaceutical, and entertainment sectors. All the time we become unhappier, and as we become unhappier, instead of beginning the journey to find purpose and fulfilment, we turn to antidepressant drugs. In doing so, we stuff the pockets of drug companies. Can you see the massive problem facing us?

The Discovery
Reflection and Purpose

What Does Your Life Mean?

I am a passionate believer that the ability to be genuinely open-minded to choice is absolutely essential to the development of the individual and to the health of society as a whole.

I believe that in limiting your life choices and being inflexible in your worldview—whether this be in connection with the opinions you hold and the opinions of others you respect; the people you choose to surround yourself with; the philosophies, politics, and religions you choose to accept and reject; and the parameters you place on your own capabilities and potential—not only are you pouring water on the creative flame that burns inside you but also you are depriving the world of the real you in all your glorious and pure form.

With this said, somewhat counter-intuitively, I want to ask you a question and provide you with just three possible options, of which only one can be your answer. Please read each of the below statements and, being as honest as you can, choose the one that best describes you, even if only loosely. Your answer will provide you with a baseline from which to work, one that we will be able to build on as we progress through the rest of the book and add more context.

Remember, be brutally honest in your answer.

1. I know what is the truth, and I am staunch in my beliefs. I spend time only with those who also share my opinion of the truth and who have the

same belief structures. I am wary of engaging with those who disagree with me. In fact, often I detest them for their views. I believe that my belief system is correct, and I often shout to the world about my superior moral virtue.

2.   I feel to a large degree that my life is being dictated to me by society. I do not have the opportunities that I want, nor do I know how to find them. I can feel time ebbing away, but I am increasingly accepting of my averageness and ordinariness. I have regrets from the past and am fearful for the future. But I tend to follow the rules because it's easier.

3.   I realise the importance of learning and growth every day. I am striving to find my authentic voice, personality, and way of life. I am curious and fascinated by the world around me. I may have had struggles and been through traumatic times, but I know these experiences shaped me into who I am. I am not scared of life. I am still suffering, but I derive understanding from this suffering and use this understanding to develop as an individual and to serve society. I believe I can achieve great things and leave a legacy when I die.

Statement 3 relates to what I believe is the most important concept in human existence: purpose.

I want to show how living a life according to ideology (see statement 1), or alternatively to be beholden to the perceived rules of society (see statement 2), is a recipe for unhappiness, frustration, depression and, given the current circumstances, moral depravity and that the only path to true fulfilment is to strive for purpose by cultivating values and ideas and making brave choices. I want to argue that the only real antidote to feelings of depression, anxiety, and worry is the quest for meaning. I want to contend that we are living in a period in human history where the importance of individuals finding their own unique meaning in the face of growing group orthodoxy, hostility, madness, and widespread narrow-mindedness is essential for the future livelihood of our world. And finally, I want to stress that the only way we can achieve any of this is by developing our own ideas and rejecting doctrinal thinking.

The Pursuit of Power or the Resignation to Dulling Conformity?

Have you ever considered your relationship towards the notion of power? If I asked you whether your life so far was defined more by the willingness to gain power over your own character or the itch to exercise power over others, how would you honestly answer? I would argue that one of the main reasons why the Western world finds itself in such turmoil is because there are too many who have chosen pursuit of power over others rather than power of introspection. I see the ruthless pursuit of wealth, status, and control over others at any cost all around, at a macro level such as in politics but also at a micro level such as the workplace.

It may be theoretically possible for top-down government control to energise and inspire societies and populations in a way that liberates and empowers them, but this can be done only if the individuals comprising that society value their freedom and right to self-autonomy to a large enough degree. If those individuals are not sufficiently awake to keep those in power in check, then the danger lies in charlatans being able to dupe and con their way to unfettered power with false promises and seemingly positive intentions that turn out to be completely insincere. Once in a place of undiluted power, these tyrants are exceptionally difficult to challenge, and the system is fiendishly difficult to change. Tyrants, together with the tyrannies they preside over, require an exhaustive effort over a long period of time from many millions of people to remove, as we are currently experiencing. Many are the individuals who want to achieve their selfish objectives without so much as a nod to the effect it may have on others around them or their environment. These individuals are numerous across the world. Those who strive for power over others usually display traits of narcissism, ignorance, psychopathy, arrogance, and absence of emotional intelligence, and they are inherently dangerous, regardless of the environment in which they operate and the number of individuals over whom they hold sway. You will probably be aware of contemporary prominent politicians, scientists, and heads of non-governmental organisations, technology, and pharmaceutical cartels who clearly fall into this category, but it is also more than likely that you have encountered these types of people in your own life.

The overarching thing that those addicted to power understand that others don't is that society's hierarchical structure can relatively easily be exploited for their own ends and that the unfortunate masses, burdened by their limiting beliefs, narrow perception, and inability or unwillingness to realise their own innate potential or express their authentic personality, are unable to do anything about it. It is, therefore, a responsibility of all who are in some way aware of how power dynamics work to stop those who wish to wield power using Machiavellian objectives from doing so. This is ensured by these same people pursuing higher purpose personal values such as authenticity, courage, integrity, freedom, and truth (see later for more about the importance of personal values). Indeed, the individuals who want to shine and find what they are capable of but whilst doing so are also introspective, open-minded, respectful of others, and aware of those around them are the ones who provide real value to society and are the cherished individuals who will lead our world back from the brink of darkness and into the light. These are the people who are celebrated in this book.

In contrast to those who are hooked on gaining, maintaining, and increasing power are those who feel stifled, paralysed, or otherwise mired in a never-ending cycle of confusion and inertia. They may or may not be suspicious of those who want or who do control them, but they struggle to discern their own purpose and sense of direction. So why do people in their millions not properly reflect on their unhappy lives? Why do they not take the time to find out where they are in life? Why do they not explore their own gifts? Why do they not try to explore what greatness they could potentially achieve? Why do they choose safety instead of adventure? Why do they neglect all of these things and instead consign themselves to a life of tedious conformity and numbing convenience? We come back again to that word: meaning. They either have no appetite to find the meaning in their lives, or they have never been taught how to.

During the rest of this book, I want to explore why this may be and what we can do about it.

You Are the Antidote to the Insanity of the Mob

Small-mindedness, spitefulness, and narcissism, fed by an accelerating authoritarianism, has spread like a poison in Western society. At the root of this is a terminal disease of the collective mind, body, and soul. The sickening symptom of the disease means that society holds the state and the group in much higher esteem than the individual. Groupthink is trumping individual opinion, and the angry, brainwashed mob is in full, rasping voice. Increasingly, the only individuals who are valued are the ones who reflect prevailing opinion or who voice the 'correct' views, whether they be on politics, religion, gender, science, or whatever. The result? People in their millions are hesitant to explore and find meaning in their lives for fear of isolation, ridicule, and disdain. This is a contemptible and highly dangerous position in which the world finds itself. We have a situation whereby people with ruthless ambition to create a world according to their own nefarious values are gaining control over an unquestioning, compliant population and are leading society towards permanent, horrific, and unprecedented totalitarianism.

Throughout history, society has flourished and been enriched far more by the gifts of individuals rather than group action or government decisions. Whether it be historical figures in art, literature, science, philosophy, or sport, beautiful creations that act as an inspiration to millions and leave a legacy for future generations are nearly always offered by *individuals*. They are able to do this because they have walked the path to finding true meaning in their lives, a path that has resulted in them unearthing a unique gift that nobody else could have bestowed upon the world. This is why it is essential that as many of us as possible try to find the meaning in our lives, regardless of how difficult, risky, and lonely the journey may be. My own longing for meaning has led me to writing this book. It might not sell, it may not be popular, and it could disappear into obscurity. What matters is that it helps me to make sense of the world, to make sense of myself, and to find meaning in my life.

I sincerely hope you do take value from this book and that it inspires you in some way to find the meaning you long for in your own life.

Did We Completely Miss the Point?

On 14 February 1990, one of the most famous and impactful photographs ever taken was made available for the public to see. Named *Pale Blue Dot*, it was taken by the Voyager 1 space probe, which at that time had travelled 3.7 billion miles into outer space. The image showed Planet Earth as a micropixel, barely visible against a backdrop of black nothingness. The photograph became famous because it was able to demonstrate the incomprehensibly miniscule size of Earth set against the unfathomable vastness of our universe. This photograph was important because it taught those who wanted to learn something critically important: that when set against the celestial heavens, we are insignificant. It allowed us to reframe how we view our existence, our lives, our condition, and our appreciation and understanding of space and time. For those who understood, it inspired, confused, provoked awe, and provided a new and critically important perspective.

Why am I talking about this photograph? Because I feel that humanity has largely missed the lesson that it offered us. The science and technology required to launch a probe deep into space, communicate with it, and receive a photo taken by it despite it being 3.7 billion miles away was a testament to human ingenuity. But the real point relating to consciousness, experience, and life itself was overlooked. Instead of a humbling re-examination of who we are, why we are here, and what all this means, society continued on its relentless journey towards scientific and technological progress at all cost. Instead of an acknowledgement that there are an infinite number of ways to see the world, interpret them, and respond to them, we chose to be omnipotent in our own little way. Perched on this tiny blue planet in what we currently understand to be a void of eternal lifelessness, we weren't awestruck, we weren't captivated, and we weren't humbled. We rejected wonder, discovery, and eternity, and instead we strove for safety, certainty, and utopia.

Life is a Tragicomedy

Death stalks us permanently as our constant silent companion, waiting to scoop us in its embrace. In acknowledging this truth, we can start to make peace with the reality that we are on this speck of dust in a never-ending universe for merely a stitch in time. This, if we just allow it, instructs us to live our best life and become who we really are. Begin to strive for and live through meaning, and life becomes abundant whilst fears melt away. Each one of us was transported from an unknowable and mystifying realm to this world and state of consciousness for a few decades before we will again return to that mysterious place, far beyond the comprehension of the human mind. Why not make the most of it whilst we are here? Do we really need to be so scared?

And yet the Western world seems to have found itself stranded in a barren wasteland, somewhere between life and death. Many are in a stifling purgatory here on Earth, one where life cannot be properly embraced for fear of inviting death and where existence, however humdrum and colourless, is all there is. It seems that we have forgotten what the essence of life actually is— a tragedy playing out alongside a comedy, heartbreaking yet hilarious. And it is precisely because of that tragedy, heartbreak, and darkness that we see the flame of incredible beauty, love, and hope burning incandescently. The sadness is ultimately worth bearing in order to experience the incomprehensible joy that life gives us. We must try to remember this before it is too late.

Who Am I?

Every individual asks themselves, 'Who am I?' intermittently and often frequently in their lives. The question drives some to self-discovery, some to confusing inertia, and some to destruction and death. As a starting point for answering this question satisfactorily, consider this quote by American psychologist Abraham Maslow: 'If you plan on being anything less than you are capable of being, you will probably be unhappy all the days of your life.'[9] Indeed, to receive a message from the soul—a deep knowing—instructing you to pursue your life mission and to ignore that message, with all the associated guilt and shame, is the greatest burden of all for one to bear.

What else is at the root of Maslow's observation? It is this essential question: Are you willing to get to know yourself? Put even more simply, are you willing to educate yourself?

---

[9] Abraham Maslow.

Education as a Doctrine

I talk about education in a personal and introspective sense, not a conventional one. I talk not of the education churned out by schools, colleges, and universities but of knowledge of self. In fact, the traditional education system has much to answer for in not preparing children and young adults for the challenges they will encounter in life. Perhaps this is the real point of its existence.

Worse, academia as a whole, but universities in particular, are guilty of massively narrowing minds. This is the very opposite of their supposed purpose. Radical politics has become established on campuses in the United Kingdom and United States with an insular, intolerant, and regressive political agenda behind much of what is taught, debated, and accepted. And in this we see a prime example of ambitious, dangerous individuals wielding their power and influence for ideological and often selfish ends. It is shocking to see what is happening at universities in the modern day. The scale of the illiberal culture that has scandalously been allowed to take root and fester unchallenged is truly frightening.

Positive education is about being able to discuss the ideas given to us and expanded upon by the great authors, philosophers, and creators of the ages and arguing for and against their relative merits. It is not about ruthlessly demolishing their ideas and offerings in favour of pursuing untested and divisive critical race and gender theory and woke ideological agendas. Positive education is also about looking inwards and using our powers of contemplation and self-examination to ask, then answer, the question, 'Who am I'? However, universities and student unions, with their no-platform policies, student safe spaces, warped and unrepresentative political agendas and manifestos, and constant streams of propaganda, do little, if anything, to encourage a discourse around either of these notions. Instead, we see increasing numbers of hung-up, indoctrinated students leaving university with narrowed minds and neurotic outlooks. It takes a truly enlightened young person to rise above all of this and derive the actual education they feel they need before moving on to the next phase of life. I would implore and discourage any young person from going to university (with notable exceptions in areas which do require a specific degree) and instead look to alternative forms of education, of which there are many. It is no exaggeration to say that the Western educational model, with its emphasis on obedience and conformity, has failed (or, if looked at from another angle, succeeded). Indeed, we see proof of this right now in the sheep-like behaviour and cowardly outlook of many.

So if not traditional education, then what?

Self-Reflection is the Starting Point

It seems to me that introspection is a trait sadly lacking in today's Western world because we have been conditioned to disconnect from our true spiritual essence. Life, with all of its stresses, pressures, need to conform, need to compare, and fixation on material goods and money, is very mind dominated. People have become lost in a maze of confusing and unhelpful thoughts, trapped by expectations and fears about what may happen if the life template they have adopted is not adhered to correctly or the societal endorsed path not properly traversed. Worst-case scenarios, similar to those peddled constantly by the media, also plague the existence of many individuals. Many worries relate to loss of job, loss of livelihood, or loss of reputation, yet often these fears are irrational and a result of being trapped in the perceptual prison talked of earlier. Is it really beyond the realm of fantasy, considering we live in a world with infinite possibility, that there may be a way to more prosperity, more contentment, and more purpose by choosing a different path to the one currently walked? I understand the predicament, as I was once in a similar situation, aware that I needed to change my circumstances but struggling to take the step. When I finally walked away from the claustrophobia and oppressive environment of my former workplace, I instantly felt a sense of true liberation. Like an animal released from its cage and into the wild, I was once again free.

What, therefore, is the solution to this dilemma that so many face? It lies in the practice of self-reflection, realisation, and action. Only in exploring the reasons that underpin the fear of loss of job, livelihood, or reputation can we begin to rationalise those fears. Only in opening our minds to our own potential and greatness can we start to appreciate the plethora of opportunities that await us. Only by taking true responsibility for being who we really are can we set about unlocking our unique gifts and offer them to a society much in need. One of the many things that should be taught in school, but isn't, is how to live intuitively. We have become so detached from our inner god that intuition is a concept often viewed with an air of suspicion or cynicism. And yet it is intuition, with its heart-centred knowing, that is our true guide in life. The mind may be clever, but real intelligence lies in the heart. Anybody who is in any way in tune with their intuition would have been able to feel that things were not as they were portrayed when the COVID situation presented; their gut instinct would have instructed them.

Prior to 2020, one of the main narratives in society, highlighted particularly by the media, universities, and celebrities, was concerning mental health. (Incidentally, it is no surprise to me that the conversation around mental health has largely disappeared since the advent of the COVID era, leading me to the conclusion that many of those public figures passionately advocating for improved mental health services and better conversations didn't really care at all. After all, why focus on mental health when there is so much virtue signalling to get involved in regarding mask wearing, lockdowns, and jabs?) However, in my opinion, the debate around it was always hopelessly flawed. It focussed almost exclusively on just one part of the solution—support—and ignored the other part, introspection. Unfortunately, one does not work without the other. This is merely a reflection of society at large, one that neglects personal responsibility in favour of external management, solutions, and control. Enlightenment can be reached only with a willingness to look deeply into the soul, to find the rotting branches on the tree of life and cut them away, and to peel away the layers of decay in order to access the true fruits of existence. One of the most fundamental lessons I have learned in my life is this: The answer, should you wish to find it, is always within.

A Well-Lived Life Needs Values

I have talked extensively in this book about the values of our age being poor and not conducive to building a society that is strong in mind, spirit, and emotional intelligence. But how about values when applied to the individual? The clarity I have gained in my life since identifying which values are essential to me is astounding. Until being introduced to the immense importance of unearthing what these values were, I had no idea of the power and sense of purpose I was able to derive. I now try to imbue my life, love, and work with these values, and I regularly reflect on them to see with which values I am in alignment and to which I am not paying enough attention.

When I look around, I think it is easy to tell which individuals have made an attempt to identify their higher purpose values and which haven't. Many are still staggering around supermarkets with masks on, sunken-eyed, weary, and imprisoned by fear. This is despite the mask mandate being lifted (at the time of writing this chapter) and a mass vaccination programme designed to offer the solution to the threat that they were initially made to fear. Some are subjugating themselves still further by wearing masks outside. Have these people ever made an attempt to understand their bizarre behaviour, and what may be underpinning their fears? Others are refusing to countenance the awful situation that the world currently finds itself in, burying their heads in the sand and wishing it will all go away, without taking proactive steps to help those who are providing resistance and attempting to find solutions. Have they ever tried to understand what explains their fear of taking responsibility, engaging with the problem, and choosing to be part of the solution? The answer, I would confidently assert, is no, and the reason is probably because they haven't identified their life values. They may be nice people, but here's the real question: Are they good people? Moreover, what happens when the next large-scale media fabricated threat materialises, as it inevitably will? Is their response likely to be the same—namely capitulation, submission, subservience, and blind obedience to government orders in the face of manufactured fear? Sadly, I believe the answer to be yes.

Similarly, it is shocking that so many in positions of authority or influence have abandoned their professional values in the last couple of years. For example, have all doctors and nurses really been pursuing values such as honesty, integrity, and altruism when dealing with patients? Have all teachers been acting with respect, care, and selflessness towards their pupils? Have all journalists been seeking truth, impartiality, and accuracy when reporting on events? Have all police officers been displaying courage, compassion, and dignity when interacting with the public? Have all politicians been protecting, listening, and serving their people? Have all scientists been approaching their work with open-mindedness, scepticism, and creativity? How many individuals within these professions have imbued their work with these crucial values, and how many have sacrificed them all too easily? It gives me no pleasure at all to say that I believe history will reflect appallingly on the health, teaching, and journalistic professions in particular for their complicity in one of the worst crimes ever committed against humanity.

One of the interesting observations I have made during the last couple of years is that those who have actually made a stand against rising tyranny—whether in researching and sharing, creating and influencing, and peaceful non-compliance and civil disobedience, or all three—often have things in common. They may have suffered addiction, depression, or PTSD; many have small, independent businesses; and others are very connected to the natural world and spiritually attuned. In all cases, whether understanding and dealing with psychological problems, deciding how the product or service that a business offers will help its customers, or wanting to introspectively learn about their small but important place in the grand scheme of life, a set of values is the key to access the door of realisation.

My top ten values, in descending order of importance, are truth, freedom, balance, self-care, gratitude, responsibility, discipline, self-awareness, open-mindedness, and perspective. Some of these values, such as truth and freedom, I feel fully aligned to, whilst others, such as self-care and discipline, I am not. Having this list of carefully defined values is instructive in that I am able to determine what is important to me and see the areas where I am living authentically and those where I am not. Taking the recent examples into account informs me that I am striving for a world where freedom and truth are cherished, but I am not paying enough attention to my own health and routine. This is useful in that it provides me with knowledge of where I need to focus my attention. The crucial thing to remember is not that we should become imprisoned by our values but that we should use them as guiding principles for how we can live better lives.

It is also a humbling experience to look for the qualities in others that we admire. This widens our awareness even further and reminds us of how much better we can be as individuals if we seek inspiration and learn from others. In my life, I admire my girlfriend Sarah's ability to remain calm, her gift of listening intently, and her unbelievable generosity. My mum has taught me love, kindness, and tolerance, and my dad showed me the importance of loyalty, a sense of duty, and forgiveness.

Are we witnessing the collapse of modern Western civilization? If so, what comes next?

The fanatical praise of the NHS is just one indication of a society gripped by madness

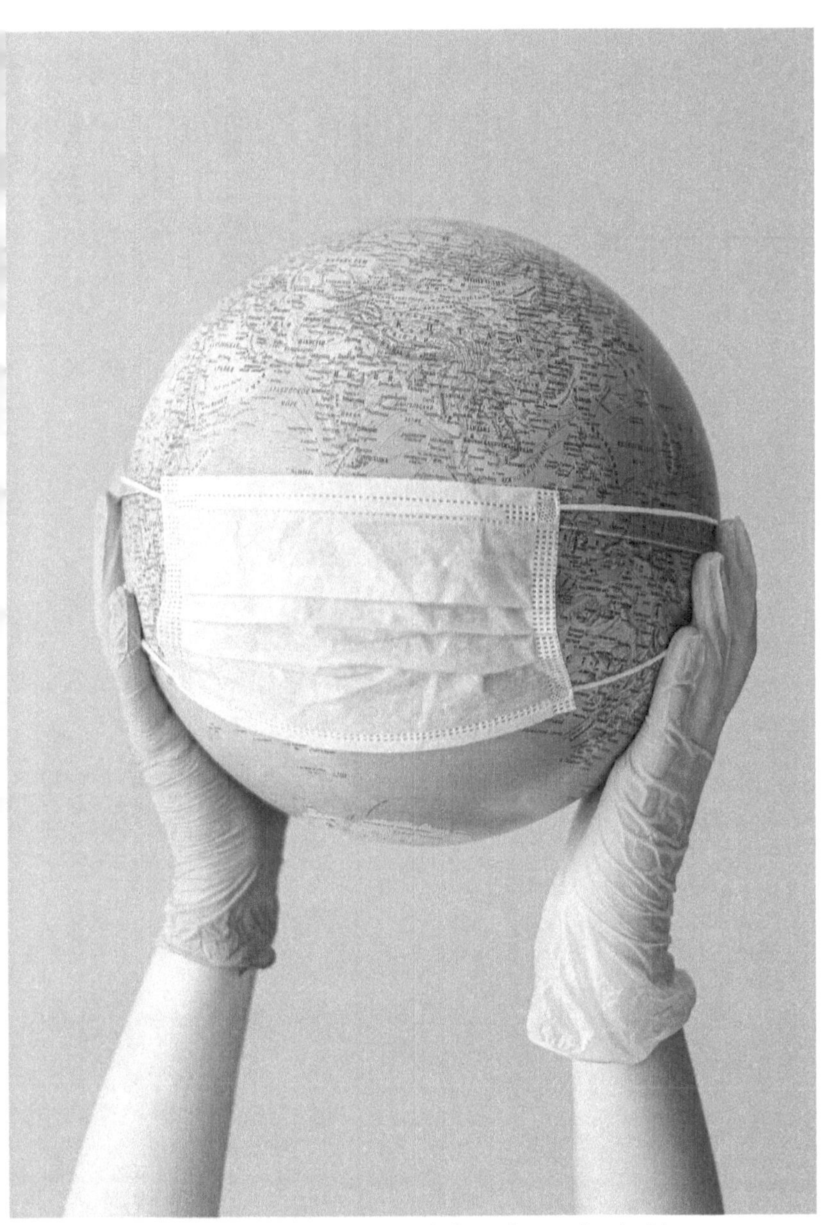

Without the relentless propaganda from the media, the bizarre behaviour of the public simply would not have happened

The censors of our age are intolerant and ruthless.

Why did so few ask questions when told to wear
a mask? (artwork courtesy of Gary Beach)

Auschwitz is perhaps the best example we have of the depths of evil of which
human beings are capable when a society is lulled into psychosis.

The brainwashing has been utterly incredible in its impact.

If God is dead, what have we replaced him with and what dangers does this pose?

Many have lived in a perceptual bubble all of their lives.

The television is the monster in the corner of the room.

Our societies have become corrupted by too
much comfort and convenience.

Just as the river ebbs and flows, so to do our lives
as we search for and pursue purpose

We exist in a realm of infinite consciousness and incompressible depth and scale (photograph courtesy of Matt Connors).

We are one with the universe. What does your intuition tell you? (photograph courtesy of Matt Connors)

But, social justice warrior, do you practice what you preach?

Falling prey to groupthink results in an ever narrowing of minds (artwork courtesy of Gary Beach)

It may be lonely at first, but we must pursue
meaning by walking our own unique path.

The spiritual awakening is real and
is wholesome and powerful.

Open minds and open hearts are what this world needs.

Is the sun rising or setting on our age?

What is the Universe Telling You?

Are you feeling sad, lonely, or depressed? If so, it is likely that you are ready to find true meaning in your life. Being depressed, anxious, worried, or consumed by neurotic thought is your subconscious telling you that something in your life needs to change, whether that be a destructive habit, a limiting or long-held belief, or your environment. Every fibre of your being is screaming at you that things are not in alignment and that a pattern interrupt is required. This manifests itself through intense feelings of mental, and sometimes physical, suffering and anxiety. It may be that these feelings have intensified significantly in the last couple of years as the world around you seems to have descended into unfathomable chaos and turmoil, possibly imbuing your situation with a massive sense of urgency. I truly believe that depression and anxiety are nature's way of sending you a signal, one that you may understand on a deeply subconscious level but are unable to unravel at the surface. The signal is instructing you to become you, no matter how difficult the process may be. It means you have far from given up on yourself. On the contrary, you are open to finding the meaning in your life. When I earlier asked you to choose a statement that best represents you, it is possible that you answered numbers 1 or 2, yet you feel unease, worry, and sadness. Do not worry; deep down, you are longing to find meaning. And right now, this wounded world desperately needs you to do so.

There is another crucially important point to make here relating to suppression. Could it be that you feel depressed because you are suppressing an important part of your true character? If so, what is this, and have you considered the potential disastrous effects that may eventually play out not only for you as an individual but also for society generally? This is a society that I believe comprises many individuals suppressing their real selves. Media-spun narratives have become more powerful in recent years, workplaces are more dictatorial and regimented, and candid conversations in many environments are generally avoided as the prevailing winds blowing through our world are ones of safety, risk aversion, and offence culture. It is natural, therefore, that many individuals have found themselves sacrificing aspects of their character for fear of being singled out or shunned by family, friends, or their boss. A society with too many people self-censoring or otherwise scared to live in accordance with their real life values is one that is doomed. If you fall into this category, your own sanity and health, as well as that of society, rests on you doing what you know is right.

Authenticity and Finding Meaning

In my own life, I spent years depressed and procrastinating. Very small but intense periods of optimism, creativity, and productivity were interspersed between long periods of deep unhappiness and inner tumult. The outwards manifestation of this was a propensity to sleep for many hours during the day to avoid the challenges facing me followed by frequent bouts of heavy drinking and gambling to anaesthetise myself against the world. Looking back, I can see that my state of mind, outlook, and behaviour were as a result of one thing: my struggle to be my authentic self. I was suppressing who I really was due to a combination of social conditioning and an unwillingness to take responsibility. I was aware that I needed to find meaning in my life and the world, even if I may not have understood this compulsion as I do now, but I did not understand that my lack of true authenticity was the major reason in stopping me from pursuing that meaning.

I can see now how I was aware from a very early age on a subconscious level (and latterly most definitely on a conscious one) that social convention, expectations, and pressures, whether via parents, environment, media influences, or the education system, were harmful to my sense of true self. This led to feelings of hopelessness, isolation, and often despair as I struggled to impose myself on the world in a way that I really wanted to. From very early on, I noticed a laziness and selfishness in my own personality, traits that I am still working to improve, but I always knew I was open-minded and willing to take risks. In others, I noticed, and continue to notice, a scepticism and an unwillingness to ever leave the comfort zone borne out of a fear of breaking from society's trap of conformity. I can now see that even though I did not know it at the time, I was starting to form my own set of values in order to find my authentic self and derive that precious meaning.

This isn't to say that I haven't been blessed with my life, because I have been, truly. My wonderful parents, my family, and my upbringing and environment were key factors in making me the person I am today, and I have learned from much wisdom and knowledge. I am deeply grateful for the positive, loving people in my life. Without them, I would not be writing this book.

Being Authentic in an Inauthentic World

In this Orwellian world, dishonesty, deception, falseness, and manipulation permeate many facets of society. Can you see through it? By standing out as genuine and unique, great opportunity awaits.

Let's start with social media. Facebook and Instagram tell us more about ourselves as we really are than the actual real world does. It shows how shallow, empty, and soulless we have become. Take one look at the average Facebook profile and witness a money-orientated world of sandy beaches, holidays, cocktails, and happy times. Compare that to the real world and see lives far removed from that which are portrayed online. It appears to offer proof that money, wealth, and status are the values that must be aspired to at the cost of all else. Who people might become if they reflected on this disingenuous way of life is meaningless because for many, they have committed to this make-believe world and are lost forever. Facebook is a monster, consuming its victims bit by self-loathing bit. And in their masses, people conform to the expected behaviour online: leave your real self at the door, live an on-screen life of 'let's pretend', switch on that Instagram filter, tell yourself that the hundreds of artificial 'friends' really matter, and most crucially, never discuss an actual idea or tell people what you really think.

The dating environment is very similar, with honesty, authenticity, and communication—three key themes in striking up and maintaining a successful relationship—completely absent much of the time. Tinder and other dating apps play on people's need for self-validation and approval, resulting in 'swipe rights' and matches being the overarching aim of the game and frustration for millions who use dating platforms in a genuine but desperate attempt to find love, only to be manipulated, made fun of, and ignored. The shallowness is extreme, and the ability to draw out narcissistic tendencies is disturbing. Again, we return to the themes of manipulation, image, and falsehood. Who is brave enough to move away from this self-loathing space with its immature, power-hungry, self-obsessed, game-playing charlatans and instead look for love in a braver, more open, more honest endeavour? Luckily for me, my beautiful girlfriend, Sarah, is one of these people. I am truly lucky to share my life with someone who is courageous, wise beyond her years, honest in the way she communicates, and true to herself and her values.

We see pretence and deceit in the way many words are now used. 'Tolerance', 'progressive', 'equality' 'inclusion' and 'liberal' are just five words that have been hijacked and whose meanings have been inverted. They now serve mainly as politically motivated buzzwords used by people who live their lives and shape their outlook in a completely incongruous manner to the true meaning of the word. It's so easy to see through these people that it's almost comical! Next time you hear somebody preaching about tolerance, strike up a conversation with them and see how tolerant they really are. We live in a world where intolerant social media celebrities and their hangers-on preach the values of tolerance. Politicians and company bosses publicise how they strive for progressive changes to society and the workplace, yet they implement regressive policies and rules. Journalists brainwash people about equality yet slyly and deceitfully create and perpetuate narratives that promote massive inequality. Insular characters sing the praises of inclusion yet respect only the right type of person with the correct viewpoint. Talking heads champion liberalism but behave in blatantly illiberal ways. And so it goes on—a never-ending quagmire of subterfuge, deception, and hypocrisy.

We see a lack of authenticity all around us in materialistic lifestyles built around money rather than fulfilment, in weddings used as occasions for the married couple to flaunt themselves and their (often fictitious) wealth, in unethical and immoral business practices and charities, in politicians with devious and malevolent objectives, in high-minded and spiteful social justice warriors proposing tyrannical and ignorant solutions to complex problems, and in scheming and cunning characters in the workplace. Fake is all around. It defines our time. The world needs authentic people with the courage to find their meaning as never before. Set against this background, can you see the unbelievable opportunity you have if you can find the meaning in your life and determine your unique purpose in this world? Can you see how you will stand out like a beacon? Can you summon up the necessary courage, face down the zealots, stand tall, and discover who you really are? Are you ready?

Entitlement versus Individual Responsibility

A sense of entitlement is the scourge of our age and is the saboteur of the attempt to find authenticity and fulfilment. Napoleon Hill, in his 1937 book *Think and Grow Rich*, written in the aftermath of the 1929 Wall Street crash and subsequent catastrophic global recession, offers this thought: "The world depression brought the opportunity you have been waiting for. It taught people humility, tolerance and open-mindedness."[10] Humility, tolerance, and open-mindedness. Three qualities sorely lacking in today's world. Why? Could it be that we have recently lived through the longest period of peacetime in many years and that, whilst making us the luckiest generation that has ever lived, it also makes us the most selfish, ignorant, and entitled? A staggering complacency has taken root in the Western world, a complacency so astonishingly powerful that we have handed over many of our liberties to the state without so much as a second thought. It could easily be argued that we are now in the midst of a third world war, one waged by governments on their citizens using information and propaganda and characterised by contradiction, confusion, and a never-ending sense of threat.

It is a damning indictment of human nature that, when taken to its natural end, the only way to promote peace is through war. True perspective for many societies only arises via death, bloodshed, misery, and suffering. Tyranny is enabled when those in power, driven by an insatiable thirst for more power, slowly alter the fabric of society so that positive values such as humility,

---

[10] Napoleon Hill, *Think and Grow Rich* (Ralston Society, 1937).

tolerance, and open-mindedness are no longer treasured as values essential to a highly functioning society. A drip feed of propaganda, spread via policy, misinformation, doublethink, the media, and the education system, slowly programmes the population that the values of yesterday are the antithesis of what the values of today and tomorrow should be. Attempts are made to rewrite history, a narrow-minded herd mentality slowly assumes initiative over independent thought, and a nebulous cloud of repression descends. Slowly but surely, those in power enable the conditions whereby an unaware and mostly unquestioning people sleepwalk its way into darkness. We need only look at the insane period of time starting from February 2020 to see an unarguable example of this. The public has largely accepted the state's taking of their most basic freedoms, abided by the intolerable lockdowns and acted on the instructions that they must subject their bodies to an experimental vaccine that is quite clearly and demonstrably not safe.

A wilful ignorance, as unforgivable as it is dangerous, has consumed us. We have become so cosseted, so far removed from the horror of war and dictatorship, and so oblivious of the capacity of humankind to unleash hell on earth that we have taken complete leave of our senses. We were so lucky and entitled that we could no longer even conceive of such things. It is lamentable. At the very heart of all of this is a collective absolution of individual responsibility—a responsibility to take heed of the lessons of the past; a responsibility to not reshape history to make it conform to preferred ideals and ideologies but to judge it impartially based on facts; a responsibility to respect and protect democracy; a responsibility to make value judgements on people, situations, and events as we see them and not how we wish them to be seen; a responsibility to uphold the right of every person to voice their opinion; a responsibility to find our unique place and purpose in the world and offer value to our communities; and a responsibility to reject the myopia and paranoia of the group in favour of self-discovery and meaning.

The greatest responsibility of all has been shirked by many, which is the responsibility to protect the next generation so they too can enjoy the rights and freedoms that we once held: freedom of speech, expression, and association; right to bodily autonomy; and right to live in a world free from constant tyranny, coercion, propaganda, and censorship. Parents in particular must ask themselves some difficult questions. It appears to me that so many parents have absolved themselves of the responsibility to ensure their children don't grow up in a world full of fear, danger, and lost opportunities. How can this be so?

As with inauthenticity, we see entitlement everywhere we look. We see it in the refusal to accept the results of democratic events (look no further than the last two US elections and, even more strikingly, the vote for Brexit), we see it in the misguided belief that happiness is a right, we see it in the money-for-nothing welfare culture that has become entrenched in the Western world, we see it in the inability to be exposed to or engage with opinions that may be different to the ones held, and we see it in the right to not be offended. A sense of entitlement is the destroyer of people's capacity for charity, positive change, and the seeking of meaning. And this sense affects millions of people across the world. Entitlement should have no place, if you want to make a difference to your own life and the lives of those around you.

The Quest
Storytelling and Evolution

Groupthink is the Enemy of Meaning

What is the reason behind this surge in entitlement ethos? I believe it has arisen in tandem with the surge in groupthink ethos and its hopelessly flawed hierarchical structure, which is obsessively based on group identity. This neo-Marxist way of arranging society is driven by ideologically fixated politicians, the media, Hollywood, academia, the public sector, and establishment-backed social movements such as Black Lives Matter, Stonewall, and Extinction Rebellion. People are no longer valued for who they are as individuals but are categorised according to what group they fall into. Depending on what group they belong to, they are either the oppressor or the oppressed. The hierarchy is incredibly well defined, placing individuals in the pecking order according to their religion, race, gender, sexuality, and social status. If they are oppressed, they are automatically a victim. This dysfunctional system also creates a narrative whereby any person low down on the scale (i.e., a victim) is by default honourable and is held to different standards than others in different groups who are higher in the imaginary hierarchy.

And there we have it. We now live in a polar opposite world to the one that Martin Luther King Jr envisioned and battled to bring into reality, one where humans are not judged by the content of their character but by their skin colour, the God they worship, their biology, their choice of partner, and their social role. This is so backwards, so damaging, and so retrograde that it is not befitting a twenty-first-century society. It is easy to see, set in this context, how an expectation of entitlement has become entrenched. To be part of one of the virtuous oppressed groups low in the hierarchy provides a ready-made excuse to play the victim. Entitlement due to a sense of victimhood is an irrational state of mind borne out of an eagerness to commit oneself to the group due to an incapacity to look inwards for answers to life's challenges. In positively affirming oneself to a group, an admission has been made. It goes like this: "I too, like all of you others in this group, am a victim! I too am oppressed! I too deserve to have my problems solved!" And herein lies the issue with membership of an ideologically driven group. The capacity for developing emotional intelligence ebbs away, and an insular, entitled, and usually aggressive tribalism takes its place.

Throughout the history of humankind, tyrants have sought to wield their power by manipulating the masses using deceit, ruse, and falsehood. We see this right now, with self-righteous, despotic individuals promoting themselves as visionaries to sell an ideological dream, one where a utopian world awaits for those who say the right things, hold the correct kind of view, but most importantly are ready to have their soul blackened in order to benefit the 'common good'. The price for the group members to pay for realising this perfect world? Sell your identity to the group and never ask for it back. And heaven forbid if you stray from this pre-ordained righteous orthodoxy. Hell will rain down on you.

Join the Crowd if You Want to
Lose Your Mind and Soul

This brings us to the big question: Why are so many willing to be drawn to the crowd? The answer lies in the concept of manipulation. Some individuals aspire for power and realise it in the manipulation of the crowd in order to impose their ideas on them. Others, hopelessly trapped in a perceptual bubble which instructs them to remain ordinary and conform yet still seeking something meaningful to attach to, fall for the charisma of the manipulator and are willing to be a slave to their ideology, often at great personal cost. In being a slave to the ideology, they sacrifice their own character at the altar of conformity. A seed of an idea is sown by the manipulator along with the promise of a better world, and in striving for this better world, the convert must sacrifice their fundamental human rights, forgo their ability to think independently, and instead behave, communicate, and interact in accordance with a prescribed set of unbending rules. In seeking a truth that does not exist, they become blind to the lie. The biggest lie of all is the lie which says that the crowd knows the truth.

Of course, throughout history, crowds have on occasion acted with wisdom and insight, and in these cases a better world has been brought about via sheer numbers and willpower. History provides us with examples of tyrannical dictators being brought down by their people's refusal to go along with the lie any longer. Indeed, during the COVID-19, era millions of principled and courageous individuals across the world have congregated in towns and cities and demanded that their voices be heard.

However, this is always as a result of people making the decision to take back their freedoms in the form of civil disobedience on an individual level. In these instances, the group's energy and power is as a result of its members acting with true integrity and morality rather than unthinking blind ideological obedience. The key aspect to remember in the modern Western world is that people in their masses, whether through a sense of entitlement or a lack of historical, scientific, or moral perspective, are actively protesting to have their freedoms curtailed or doing nothing to take back those they have already lost. They have been manipulated to think that there is a path to greater abundance and even utopia by blindly following the orders of the group manipulator, ignoring the fact that what they have already lost was precious. They hold out a lock and chain and say to their master, "Incarcerate me in the prison of your ideology! Free me from the task of getting to know my own mind!" Black-and-white thinking and high-minded moral vanity are nearly always two features of crowds. Why? Because this offers crowd members the opportunity to claim to be in possession of the truth and to never be questioned. It defines a herd mentality poisoned by narcissism, arrogance, ignorance, and laziness, the four enemies in the pursuit of true meaning.

Nietzsche's observation rings true: 'In individuals, insanity is rare; but in groups, parties, nations and epochs, it is the rule.' To see this with such clarity in my own country and at such close quarters is sobering in the extreme. Indeed, to maintain sanity in a world deep in psychosis, neurosis, and hypnosis is to undergo vigorous psychological, emotional, and spiritual examination every day.

How to Find Meaning

How can you find meaning? This is a question that only you can answer, but if you possess the below qualities or are open to the pursuit of them, you will begin your journey to meaning. Your answer will not be in the form of a light-bulb moment but a slow unfolding of the realisation that you are beginning to truly acknowledge and understand yourself and your place in the world. Once this process starts, you can align every action and decision to your overall vision and then watch as things start to make more sense to you. You will notice the energy inside you change to something more wholesome, meaningful, and life-affirming. Use these suggestions in conjunction with the ones given in the chapters about self-reflection and identifying your values.

1. Recognise the Flaws in Your Character and Work on Them

One of the main reasons individuals are drawn to crowds and prone to fall prey to groupthink is they are too afraid to face up to who they might be if they scratch beneath their surface personality. Membership of a large group provides identity, a means to crusade against a perceived injustice, and above all a sense of being on the right side of history. But who has ever learned anything on a protest march or in a Facebook echo chamber? And who is ever going to learn about themselves when their precious time is not given over to honest self-reflection but instead to blindly following the crowd?

Instead, start your process of finding meaning by acknowledging that you are human and are highly fallible. Be honest with yourself and identify the aspects of your character that you know you can improve. For example, in my case, I can be selfish and have a huge tendency towards procrastination. Being selfish means I am not injecting as much positivity into the world as is possible, and tending to laziness means I am compromising reaching my true potential. I am working to improve both of these traits. Writing this book goes some way towards achieving this.

Whilst remembering the above, remember to forgive yourself your mistakes because unreconciled shame associated with mistakes will eat away at your being. To a greater or lesser degree, we all have an element of Jekyll and Hyde in our make-up. We are all predisposed to making poor decisions, taking risks based on questionable objectives, and falling prey to the temptations all around us, potentially hijacking the chances of us finding happiness. Again, to use my example, I have made many errors of judgement and often sacrificed long-term fulfilment for short-term gain. Much of my life is lost in a fog of alcohol. I have made mistakes, offended people, gambled too much, and done things detrimental to my health. I am now in a position where I can still fall prey to temptations, but because I have made, and am continuing to make, an effort to make sense of my life, the occasions are less frequent, and the damage to myself and those around me is far less.

Face up to the consequences of your actions when needed, but be gentle when the temptation is to castigate yourself. Remembering that you are far from perfect is an excellent and natural base for you to begin to find your meaning. You are an imperfect individual, and you should want to stay that way.

2. Understand That You Do Not Have a Right to Be Happy

One of the main narratives in the last few decades is that we have the right to be happy. Through the power of advertising, big businesses bombard us with the message that we can have that elusive happy life if we buy their product or service. This narrative is reinforced via the poisonous influence of the entitlement culture described earlier.

The reality is that we cannot find happiness through shiny new objects, wealth, status, or even relationships. Happiness is just one of the many states that we experience as we go through life, along with anger, frustration, joy, sorrow, worry, and a myriad of others. But look inwards for answers, and you will begin to find the peace that you crave, regardless of how disturbing events are in the outside world. Wake up every morning with the attitude that you want to learn, grow, and improve. Only in making this decision each and every day will your meaning begin to unravel. Understand this concept, and the feeling of happiness will be a more frequent by-product for you.

3. Review Your Environment

One of the biggest obstacles to change, and therefore finding meaning, could be your environment. When you go to work, do you feel inspired, energised, and creative, or do you feel stressed and a sense of dread? Are you feeling trapped and claustrophobic in a culture that you want no part of? Are you being asked to do unconscionable things and follow dictatorial orders? Are you feeling guilty?

How about your relationships? Do the people in your life share your values? Is your partner in tune with what it is you are trying to do in your life? Are they supportive? Have they surprised you in the last few years with how they have responded to a societal descent into tyranny? Have they demonstrated courage and leadership, or have they hidden away? Do they take responsibility? And how about your friends? Do they remind you of past indiscretions, judge you by the old version of yourself, and deride you for your dreams? If so, are they really the friends you need in your life? Any person in your life who refuses to let you move on from mistakes, focusses on your weaknesses rather than your qualities, and tries to hold you back is projecting their own insecurities onto you. This is harmful for you on your path to meaning.

4.   Find Your Gift and Give It to the World

Anybody who tells you that you can be or do anything you want in your life is either lying or misguided. The brutal fact is that there are certain achievements that will forever be out of your reach. But you can become the greatest if you find your innate and unique talent. This is not hyperbole but true! What is your real passion in life? Are you pursuing this as your work? If not, why not? Are you really saying that you are prepared to sit in front of a computer for the next twenty, thirty, or forty years? Our time in this life is precious beyond description, so why not spend it pursuing the thing you love? You may read this and think of a number of excuses why you can't change course. You are too busy, you don't have the time, you don't have the money, or you don't want to risk what you already have. It could be that you need to change you own story. We will cover storytelling later in the book and how we can be the heroes in our own novels. However, if you fully understand the concepts related so far in this book, you may already see the possibilities ahead. All you need to do is change your perception of yourself and your world and then watch as the door opens to possibilities that you never knew existed.

5.   Be Vulnerable

Vulnerability is fearlessness. In wanting to find meaning in your life, you are likely to walk a lonely road of uncertainty, watching the masses all walking the same old road to what they think is safety and certainty. This may be isolating and frightening for a time, but just remember that in taking your own road, you are displaying courage and bravery. You are showing that you are putting yourself directly in the way of the many obstacles that will come your way, but you are prepared to overcome them.

Vulnerability is admitting mistakes. One of the main reasons that many people feel stressed in their jobs is they are fearful of making mistakes. Much of the landscape of work is infected by a culture of blame. Making a mistake is never ideal, but it is inevitable. However, admitting a mistake is actually liberating. It is an admission that you are imperfect, flawed, vulnerable, and real. This instantly takes any power away from the person wanting to make life difficult for you as a result. Of course, sometimes there are consequences arising from making a mistake. However, much of the time the consequences are insignificant, and the mistake can be corrected. There is no reason for the culture of fear in many workplaces. Next time you make a mistake at work, admit it! You will gain more respect from your colleagues.

Vulnerability is openness. If you feel sad, tell someone. There's no need to put on a brave face and fake a smile, like many of us tend to do. Doing this results in nothing other than increasing the turmoil simmering underneath. Instead, be vulnerable and show how you are feeling. This will put you in the correct mindset for dealing with the actual problem, rather than trying to conceal and run from it. This is of incredible importance right now as many are facing problems on a scale they have never before experienced.

6.   Stay Open-Minded

Remaining open-minded is absolutely crucial. It never fails to shock me how narrow-minded so many people are, many of them seemingly intelligent. It is these individuals who, when in positions of power, are the most dangerous. One of the many things I thank my parents for was that I was not indoctrinated, or even ushered, towards any particular set of beliefs. This gave me the gift of open-mindedness from an early age. Open-mindedness, together with the defence of freedom of speech and celebration of individuality, are my real passions in life. I was not politicised or brainwashed, and they never so much as cajoled me into thinking a certain way about society and how it should be. Instead, all options were possible. As a result, the way I view society and my place in it has evolved organically. Of course, like everybody else, I have my biases and allegiances, but I am genuinely open to influence from any source. At least, I hope I am. This has resulted in me having close relationships with friends and family with wildly differing viewpoints on politics, social concerns, and philosophy.

In contrast, I see so many avenues of personal development being cut off by people due to an unwillingness to examine their own prejudices. These individuals are usually the ones most vulnerable to the degenerate aims of groupthink or state control, and interestingly, they are nearly always stressed, depressed, resentful, or all three. A black-and-white, dogmatic stance on life is not one given to uncovering meaning. Realise that the pursuit of meaning lies in constantly challenging your own preconceptions and beliefs and being open to influence from unfamiliar sources. This means subjecting yourself to sources of information with which you disagree and developing relationships with people who hold differing viewpoints to your own. Rapid growth occurs when you are forced to change your perception due to new influences and interactions.

Write Your Own Story for Your Life

Stories and storytelling have bound together human civilisation and existence for millennia. Our lives *are* a story, and we are invested in the stories of other people and places. What else could explain the popular interest in current affairs, history, notable historical figures, celebrities, reality TV, sports teams, events, and anything else that captivates us?

We are interested in stories that are told to us by the media and by politicians, by parents and by teachers, by friends and by advertisers. Stories tap into our emotions and make us feel a certain way. Stories can and do hold huge power over us. They can impel people to commit truly evil acts, they can provide the narrative to acts of heroism, they can make us fall in love, buy things we don't need, and completely change the way we look at things. It is incomprehensibly tragic that in the last few years, the story of many in our confused world is that of a disease and how to avoid it at all costs. The characters in the story have forgotten how to deal with adversity, how to apply perspective, how to nurture and protect families and communities, and how to defend freedoms and healthy ways of life. In their story, they have enslaved themselves to their government, dutifully obeying all orders to remain at home, stay away from loved ones, cower behind a mask, and have an experimental and untested injection whenever their government demands it. And yet many still wait for their next instruction. The pages continue to turn, but the story is still the same— lost meaning, lost empathy, lost perspective, and lost life.

We are also fascinated by stories on a smaller scale, ones that we can feel a part of. Next time you walk past two people in a relaxed social setting (it could be a lunch break at work, in a park, or walking past you in the street) try to tune into their conversation. It is likely that the subject of conversation will be another person, and that it will be negative in nature. Stories hold an incredible sway over us in that they provide us with an element of meaning. But just as the pair gossiping over lunch about their colleague may not be painting an accurate picture of reality and are projecting only their perception and prejudice, so too do we tell inaccurate stories about ourselves.

After recovering from a severe period of depression, I had a sudden realisation that I had immense powers of resilience. Up to this point, I had looked upon myself as lacking in will. The reality was the complete opposite. Since this realisation, I have made the theme of resilience a central tenet to my existence. I draw strength from past negative experiences and my ability to overcome them, and this gives me confidence in dealing with challenges that will inevitably come my way in the future. I have also realised my potential for leadership and discovered skills of persuasion that at one time I wasn't able to recognise. When I understood this, it became my responsibility to impart my skills onto the world in the most positive way. I set up my YouTube channel, *The Imperfect Individual*, because I knew I had to share with the world my views about what was happening and why, together with an attempt to offer solutions. I would never have forgiven myself if I had failed to listen to my higher power instructing me to do this. The same concept applies to this book. If I don't write it, then who will? If not now, when?

With this in mind, what aspects of your story simply don't reflect the real you? What things are not your reality and may be holding you back? What is the first thing that comes to mind when you think about yourself? The very first thing? Now ask yourself, Do you need to reconsider this opinion of yourself? The next part of the book will offer insight into how you can create a more vibrant, expressive, exciting, and authentic story about yourself, regardless of the chaos and insanity that is churning away in the world at large.

Being a Victim is Easy

There is a story that some people tell themselves, which is that their life is in some way being dictated for them. Their story is that they are unfortunate, unlucky, and not as privileged as some others in society. This is the ultimate limiting belief—one that paves the way for a life of underachievement, frustration, resentment, anger, and regret. Of course, there is an aspect of chance in life. We are all born into different backgrounds and environments: some are born into wealth and some into poverty, some are born into peaceful and loving homes some into abusive ones, and some are dealt cruel blows by the hand of fate whilst others enjoy good luck. But we can control our thoughts, beliefs, and decisions, and we can act in accordance with these thoughts, beliefs, and decisions to shape our world. This means that all of us, whoever we may be, can choose our own journey and tread our own unique path.

Ironically, it is often those who are born into true hardship or who suffer painful ills in life who realise this, whereas those living a life of comfort and privilege take on a victim complex. Unfortunately, there is a narrative created by those in power that the reverse is true. This is nothing but an attempt to keep people more open to manipulation, less likely to develop their own viewpoint, and more easy to deceive (in other words, to dupe people into believing that they are a victim). It takes no effort or responsibility to be a victim. There are no rules in life that we will never feel at a disadvantage, never feel challenged, never feel more unlucky than the next person, and never suffer cruel luck. But in realising that life isn't fair, we can quickly move on to focussing on the positive changes that we have within ourselves to bring about. Each one of us holds the power to shape our lives according to our will.

The world owes you nothing. Realise this, and you are free. When you are liberated from this toxic belief, nothing will stop you on your journey to love, wealth, success, fulfilment—whatever you want.

The Divine
Introspection and Spirituality

You are Being Guided to the Light by an Invisible Presence

Some call it the law of attraction, and others call it a spiritual revolution. Some say they have found religion or God. Some report accessing a deeper level of consciousness while others say that they have left a three-dimensional world and are now in a five-dimensional world. Some say they have transcended reality as we know it and are immersing themselves in the energy of a new cosmos, and others say that they can feel a powerful, heightened presence. Whatever the phenomenon is, it is real, and many of us can feel it. There is a higher power, one which has always been present but which many, including myself, have not allowed into their realm of existence until now. The phenomenon is described by people from all cultures, countries, and backgrounds; it cuts across all political and religious divides; and it is becoming ever more powerful. It is tenderly whispering to all of us that if we just trust our intuition, then everything will be OK. More and more of us are paying attention and are seeing the world in greater depth, breadth, and beauty. We are learning once more to connect with each other, to live symbiotically with nature, and to allow synergy and an organic energy flow to permeate our lives. This is not only the antidote to the evil that is presently stalking this world but also the essence of an enhanced experience of what it is to be human. It is something ethereal but real, something that is not tangible but can be accessed merely by allowing ourselves to access it, something that opens the door to a state of individual and societal enlightenment. It is the very thing that will be our salvation.

I have had fleeting glimpses of this life-affirming force since I was young, but it is only recently that I have come to understand it and tap into its power. The impossible misery, confusion, heartache, sense of loss, and trepidation associated with lockdown that I experienced in spring and summer 2020 ultimately led me to a place of such deep introspection that I began to access a greater appreciation of myself and the world around me. Despite the extreme circumstances in the outside world, I started to find a sense of deep purpose, I implicitly trusted the mysterious power that was beginning to show the way, and I seized upon the responsibility that I knew had been thrust upon me. I committed myself so completely to defeating the totalitarianism that I could see was threatening to destroy the world that I felt liberated from fear and worry. All that mattered was today, and today I would take one more brick out of the wall of tyranny, however possible. The true purpose in my life had presented itself in the most unexpected manner and at the most unexpected time.

Most likely you will understand that everything I am saying is connected to perception, intuition, and awareness. These interlinked concepts combine to offer a deeper insight to a world that lies beyond what we merely see and hear. I believe there are four elements that comprise this heightened state, the first of which is aloneness. First of all, note the distinction between aloneness and loneliness. Whereas loneliness brings about states of negative feelings of isolation and seclusion (feelings which have become all too common for many in recent times), aloneness is the much more affirmative state of stillness and enlightenment. In these times of coordinated and ruthless media psychological operations, mass information, and crushing loneliness, the power of quiet reflection is immense. To allow abundance, positivity, and a sense of meaning to flow into your life, you must gain clarity on your aspirations, and only in creating space and time can you achieve this and begin to access the deep well of enlightenment that lies within.

Personally, I find that walks in the country, with only nature to keep me company, helps me to rid myself of needless negative thought patterns, and I return feeling invigorated, cleansed, and often inspired. As the old Roman proverb says, 'Walking solves the problem.' Each time, I am captivated by the way the natural world is able to arrange itself, look beautiful, and ensure everything still thrives in exactly the way it always has done for millions of years. It has a timeless and consistent splendour so pronounced that it can often seem unfathomable to the human observer. Whether it is walking, meditating, yoga, reading, or something else, just try to make it a daily ritual to find quiet. You will find yourself becoming calmer and more aware. These feelings arise as you find solitude and tap into something bigger, giving you a new sense of perspective on your life and your place in the universe.

The second element is visualisation. As discussed earlier, many in our dysfunctional world are trapped in a perceptual prison and a slave to the system that, for the majority, neither benefits them nor cares about them. They visualise the arrival of the weekend as soon as Monday arrives so they can be free for two days, they yearn for their summer holiday so they can escape the prison of their workplace and they count down the years so they can retire and access their pension. In a world of infinite and splendid possibility, is this not madness? Yet once we realise the limitations that have been imposed on us, the fears that drive our beliefs and behaviours, and how we willingly acquiesce to be someone else's slave, we can begin to envisage what we truly desire. For me, this is a world of healthy conversation and debate, one where the cry of freedom rings out through the land and individualism and bravery are cherished. It is no coincidence that this is the reality that is manifesting in my life. You really do bring into being what you imagine.

Third, remember that everything starts with gratitude. We all have the choice right now, at this critical inflection point for human civilisation, to be thankful that it is we who hold the power to decide what happens next. We can bring into reality a world of abundance, light, and love that is eminently possible if we just choose to. We can be the generation that finally throws off the chains of slavery and leads the way to a world of unprecedented freedom and wisdom. Be on guard against feelings of anger, resentment, and frustration and replace those emotions wherever possible with joy, forgiveness, and love; be truly grateful for the loved ones who hold us dear, and even give thanks to those who we may view as ignorant or cowardly, for even they can teach us.

Fourth is the necessity to take decisive action, whatever this may be. The psychological attack that has been ongoing for decades but which has intensified in the last few years has employed information as its weapon. This has created fear, uncertainty, division, and dread, but it has led to something even more pronounced, and that is inertia. I used to be mired in what seemed like a never-ending cycle of indecision, struggling to say no to people, hyper-analysing each thought that came to me, agonising about every basic decision in my life, and not committing to an outcome when I finally did make a decision. Being in a permanent state of indecision drained the energy from me and meant I couldn't allow clarity to strike. Now, I try to make each decision from a place of confidence, self-knowledge, and being in line with my values. I'm also comfortable that if I do make a wrong decision, I can put things right.

The constant flow of information is distracting many to such a degree that they seem to have forgotten that the primary source of interpreting their world is via their eyes and ears. I briefly fell into this trap in the spring and summer of 2020, attempting to process as much information as possible so I could be sure I was staying up to date with everything that was happening regarding COVID and lockdowns. One day, I had the realisation that what I was seeing with my own eyes and ears wasn't correlating to what others on various social media channels were telling me. I was fixating on their version of events too much and, like a rabbit in the headlights, felt paralysed and unable to move. Once I reminded myself that my reality and truth was what I could actually see and hear and that information was there only to supplement, challenge, or clarify my take on the world, I felt freed. Now, no matter how I feel on a particular day, I take action in order to bring my vision closer. Action, no matter how small, creates momentum and propels you on a forward path to the fulfilment you desire, delivers on the positive intention you have set, and changes the energy frequency within you in order to deliver what it is you want. The universe has a method of arranging people and events in such a way as to reward the person who has taken the time to reflect, create positive change, form a clear purpose, engineer daily goals, and then act on those goals.

What Can Children Teach Us?

We are all born as creators. Everybody holds within them the potential for creative genius. The essence of genius is the ability to create something unique that inspires others, possibly arousing in them a motivation to produce something inspirational and valuable all of their own. Why is it, then, that vanishingly few people go on to realise their potential for genius? Why are so few able to distil and unleash their own genius on the world? Why do fewer still even try?

A good starting point would be to acknowledge a widely held misconception which says in the child/ adult dynamic, the adult is by default the teacher. I have two nephews, each four years old, and a niece who is one, and all are a constant source of inspiration. It is they, more than anybody else, from whom I derive my most important life lessons. Why? Most strikingly of all, they have a limitless capacity for wonderment and are endlessly enraptured by the world around them. In this way, their imagination is constantly stimulated, and they find joy and amazement in everything they see and touch. In their world, anything and everything is possible. This is also true in our world, but it is something we have forgotten. Almost without exception, as human beings grow, develop, and begin to interact and communicate with the world around them, their limitless potential for imagination, wonder, and creativity is suppressed by their environment, upbringing, education, and influences. Finding your creative path is as much about unlearning much of what you have been taught as anything else— one of the truest signs of intelligence. Children can help us do this.

Second, their insatiable curiosity means they have a yearning to find out about the world around them. Their enthusiasm to learn, regardless of how difficult the task at hand, is uplifting and humbling. Watching the journey of both nephews struggle to first roll on to their side, then figure out how to propel themselves in a forward crawl, then take their first steps, and then learn to communicate via gestures and words was a lesson in the values of persistence, perseverance, and curiosity. I am watching my niece also undergo this incredible learning process. How many think that learning stops when they leave school, college, or university? How many think they have it all figured out when they have a nice car, a mortgage, three kids, and a job promotion? Keeping an appetite for learning is a crucial priority in this world of ever narrowing and hardening of views.

Third, they are completely non-judgemental. Not having been sufficiently conditioned and influenced by experiences, interactions, and events, they have not yet developed the ability to judge people and situations. Every situation is completely organic and natural. Life happens for them, and they are in awe of it. How liberating that must be!

Which Type of Fool are You?

Times change, but human nature does not. When Bertrand Russel said that 'the problem with the world is that the fools are so sure of themselves and the wise men so full of doubts', he was capturing this very notion. To be wise is to acknowledge that you are a fool, that you know an infinitesimally small number of all of the things there are to know, and that you are, by your very existence, ignorant. And yet in making this acknowledgement, we can make ourselves less of a fool than those who don't, and in the process we gain wisdom, perspective, and knowledge.

We appear to have forgotten that doubt and curiosity are two concepts that any high-functioning society must cherish. Instead, the levers of control have been unquestioningly handed over to pathological fools—individuals drunk on their ill-gotten power, doubtful of nothing and certain of everything, mired in their own hubris, captured by ideology and without an introspective fibre in their body. They decide the fate of nations in their daily Zoom meetings from their ivory towers, forcing their stupid rules and idiotic policies on their countrymen and women. Yet these fools forget one thing: one day, when all is said and done, they will pay a high price for their actions. Even more foolish are those who obediently follow the rules, mandates, and diktats of these individuals, for they cede their autonomy, choices, and right to live freely to fools who do not have the moral, lawful, or intellectual right to seize them. And so the rules issued by the fools become ever more ridiculous and tyrannical, and the fools following them do so ever more slavishly. Look around in your life and compare the wise fools with the obedient fools. Who is asking questions, and who isn't? Whose mind is their own? Who realises that they are a fool?

When it dawned on me that there was nobody to save me from tyranny other than myself, it was strangely liberating. I realised that the fools in power were not only idiots but were immoral to the point of evil, and that all of the organisational structures that I once had some semblance of trust in had been corrupted beyond comprehension. There was nobody coming to save the day. That was simply impossible. It was incumbent on me to save myself. Indeed, the key to overthrowing tyrants and rebuilding society lies with each individual making the right moral choices and using their personal power in the most effective way possible. The solution is simple in that it relies on enough wise fools taking imperfect but decisive action to ensure the removal of fools from power and hand back freedoms to not only the wise fools but also the ignorant ones. A society whereby the wise fools, with their questioning minds, creative impulses, altruistic intentions, and value of freedom, debate, and truth, are able to build a world that is fairer and more humane, with greater emphasis on individual sovereignty is eminently possible. The wise fools therefore have a responsibility to ensure the banishment of the power-obsessed lunatics back to the fringes of society and to coax their foolish followers back to morality and sanity. But the wise fools can save society only if they are willing to immerse themselves fully in their foolishness. This means taking risks and realising that to speak truth and live authentically in times such as these is to accept ridicule and castigation.

The wise fool understands something else of incredible importance—that the health of the individual and of society is dependent on the changing of minds, when required. As human beings, we are conditioned in a multitude of ways, and our outlooks and beliefs are shaped by whom we associate with, what experiences we have had, and what information we consume. However, partly due to ego but mainly because of the narrow-minded age in which we live, many are reluctant to admit when they get something wrong. People seem to commit to a position and then vehemently defend it, regardless of the alternative evidence and of the consequences. The individuals willing to countenance that there could be an alternative side of the argument than the one they have attached themselves to appear to be small in number. Never, in the history of human civilisation, has it been more imperative that enough of us are willing to adapt our stance when required than right now. For the health of our present society and that of the next generation, who deserve to live in a democratic and liberal world free from tyranny and coercion, enough of us must find the courage to utter the words 'I was wrong. I have changed my mind'.

The Fool is the Precursor to the Saviour

Carl Jung's idea that 'the fool is the precursor to the saviour' is profound. It describes the concept whereby a widespread willingness to engage in self-discovery, experimentation, and risk-taking opens the door to a more enlightened and courageous society. With this in mind, once more consider yourself and those around you, and observe who is engaging in this process. Who has been made fun of, particularly in the last few years? Who has risked all to say what needs to be said? Who has stood alone from the crowd and vociferously contradicted 'official' opinion? Who is the person who is most often laughed at, made fun of, or vilified? Who has been willing to look stupid in order to find truth? It is likely that it is they who understand Jung's idea most deeply. It is they who are saving themselves, and thereby their world, by being the fool.

As I continue on my path to saving myself, I must also recognise that I may have appeared, and may continue to appear, stupid in some ways. I wonder in how many ways I have been hypocritical, how many times my actions have not matched my words, and when have I contradicted my own position on a particular topic. How about this book? What makes no sense? What parts of the book are presenting confusing arguments? Do I portray myself as arrogant, ignorant, or naive—all of the things I profess to dislike? Am I ideological, even though I rail against ideology? The point is this does not matter. I am a fool and always will be, but maybe I am a little closer to becoming a fool with wisdom. Maybe I am a little closer to saving myself. Are you?

Questions for Introspection

You will have heard of the ancient Greek maxim 'Know thyself', but what does this actually mean? How do you know when you know yourself? What does life look like when you finally know yourself? My own view is that in all of human history, not one individual has gone to their grave having known themselves. Instead, I believe that the true sentiment behind the message 'Know thyself' is, 'Make an attempt to know thyself.' Put another way, it means, 'Be introspective.' The process of introspection is painful but is also a precious gift. Moreover, it is essential in the quest for meaning and contentment.

On this note, I hope that this book has succeeded in stirring up some emotion in you. If so, it has done its job because it is causing you to reflect on your own life so far. Now, I would like to ask you some further questions, which build on what we have already discussed and which you must try to answer honestly. Answering these questions will help give you greater clarity on why you are where you are and how you can move forward in the direction you choose.

1. What are the traits in others that you most dislike? Are there any of these traits that you can observe in your own character? If so, what can you do to improve these aspects of yourself?
2. Do you live in any way vicariously through another person? This could be your children or maybe a celebrity. If so, why? Do you think their achievements in their lives will be a source of

happiness to you? If so, why do you think you don't have the potential for achievements as well?

3. Do you cut yourself off from opinion and influences that you find uncomfortable because they don't fit with your worldview? If so, why?

4. Do you cultivate your own ideas about life and existence or fall in with doctrines and ideologies?

5. Do you follow rules that you know are detrimental to society? If so, why?

6. Up until this point in your life, have you striven to gain power over your own character or power over other individuals?

7. Have you ever challenged yourself about your beliefs and asked why you have those beliefs? Do your beliefs serve you? Do they serve society?

8. How much of your character are you consciously aware that you are suppressing? What fears are stopping you from expressing your true essence?

9. How do you perceive failure? Is it one of the keys to success or to be avoided at all costs?

10. In what ways, if any, have the last few years fundamentally changed the way you look at life?

11. Do you agree that suffering is inevitable in life? What have you learned as a result of your own suffering?

12. Do you share your own creations with the world, or do you tend to always duplicate or regurgitate what another person has created?

13. How conscious are you of your own moral compass? Do you regularly reflect and recalibrate it when you think it is necessary? Do you think society's moral compass is askew?

14. What is your understanding of history? Can you see any parallels with any other historical eras? Do you think society is repeating previous mistakes?

15. What does the phrase 'the human condition' mean to you?
16. To what extent do you live your life authentically? Are you comfortable and confident in expressing the true essence of your character, in as far as you understand it, or are the risks in being truly genuine too great to you?
17. What is more important to you: safety and security, or liberty and choice?
18. Do you agree that it is important to define life values? Are you aware of what your values are? Do you live in alignment with them?
19. Do you think utopia and perfection exists? What risks do you associate with striving for utopia and perfection?
20. Do you ensure you have your own house in order before you criticise others?
21. To what extent is your story the media's story? When you engage in conversation about important social or political issues, are you talking, or is it really the media talking through you?
22. Do you enjoy talking to those with whom you disagree? Do you welcome having your beliefs challenged and your views scrutinised?
23. To what extent is the conflict between when to accept and when to challenge a dilemma for you? Have you ever considered this notion?
24. Complete this sentence in your own words: 'The mainstream media exists primarily to ...'
25. When was the last time you changed your mind about something significant? Are you ever reluctant or unprepared to change your mind, even when you know that you were wrong initially?
26. In what ways are you a hypocrite in your life?
27. Do you think you will be on the right side of history? Why?

28. What do you do to propagate tyranny, and what do you do to defeat it?
29. Do you help unify people or divide them?
30. Do you ask questions, or do you always have the answers?
31. What is truth to you?
32. Have you recently done things that are unconscionable to you, simply because somebody has ordered you to do them?
33. Do you feed off negativity and gain a perverse pleasure from it?
34. Are you a wise fool or an ignorant fool?
35. Are you actively protecting the next generation's ability to be free and to choose?

Your Genius Resides within You

Every human being is born with the potential for greatness. You merely have to take a cursory glance at history to see innumerable examples of people from various backgrounds achieving astonishing success in their own lives and changing the world with their words, actions, and achievements. You can probably see people in your own life who are successful and happy because they intuitively understand the concepts in this book. They are that rare group of people who seem to have mastered life. Every habit they create is one that serves them well, every decision they make is wise and considered, and they are aligned in all areas of their life.

So why aren't more of us in this same category? As has been previously argued, for most people, their environment, upbringing, media, education, and social convention contrives to convince them that they can never reach their great potential, resulting in the majority settling for mediocrity in their lives. But if we take a closer look, it is easy to understand why people fall victim to this vortex of underachievement. From the moment we are born, we are conditioned to conform. Treading a different path to the majority leaves us open to possible ridicule, resentment, indifference, or suspicion. A well-worn road to a known but ultimately illusory destination—safety, security, certainty—has always been a popular one, but taking a new road that nobody has ever travelled before? That's terrifying. Exciting, yes, but terrifying. Living life on a different trajectory from the rest risks rejection from others and therefore feelings of isolation so it is not surprising that many give up. The pain associated with finding deep purpose is greater than the pain associated with continuing to conform, so people resign themselves to a less fulfilling, less exciting, and less impactful life. Is this you?

More pointedly, have you ever asked yourself what impact you would be able to make on the world, if only you could unlock the genius that lies within you? What if you were able to uncover this lurking brilliance and wield it to aid a world badly in need of what it is you have to offer? What if your destiny wasn't to be sat in front of a computer mired in admin and emails for eight hours a day, but instead was to create something magnificent that not only helped those who need it now but also left a true legacy for future generations? If you think what I'm suggesting is absurd, why? What if the notion that most people are ordinary and average and will never be touched by greatness is absurd, and that your genius lies within you and is waiting to be discovered if you just allow and enable it to be discovered?

The following affirmations are all indicators that something epic is stirring deep within you. If you relate to some or all of these points, it may be time for you to pay attention to the instructions you are being given by your higher self.

1.   I Am Aware of My Untapped Potential

I know deep within my being that there must be more to my life than sitting in front of a computer for fifty years and that being tied to a job I derive little or no satisfaction from, and which even may be doing me great psychological and physical harm, is draining me of the drive to find my calling. I know that I haven't scratched the surface of what is possible in my life up to this point and that, if I stay where I am now, I never will. I have an itch to do something else, something that is meaningful, and I have had it for a very long time. I do not want to settle, and I will not settle until I find the very thing in my life that I not only love but also can help others with. This tendency to not want to settle is applicable for other areas of my life as well. I also want to be my best self from a health, relationship, and spiritual perspective. I have high standards and feel uncomfortable when I know I don't meet them, which is presenting now as a gnawing guilt. I fear that the burden of my unfulfilled potential will become heavier to bear with each passing day.

2.   I Explore Opportunities

Instead of asking, 'Why?' in my life, I ask, 'Why not?' which is an indicator of my open mind. My default position when considering an opportunity is not one of cynicism or scepticism but of curiosity and interest. I know that to break free of the many societal traps discussed in this book, I need to explore opportunities that others either aren't aware of or dismiss without consideration. I know that reasons for not taking advantage of an opportunity are not usually reasons but excuses, and I am uncomfortable with making excuses. I may spend time reading and scouring the internet for an opportunity that I just know is out there waiting for me to discover, and I educate myself on money, personal development, lifestyle choices, and business. I also realise the importance of tapping into a more enlightened state of being in order to ensure I draw into my life what it is that I desire. I am prepared to wait for as long as it takes, confident in the knowledge that as long as I remain positive and curious, a door to a new world will open for me. I am ready for this massive shift in my life, so I will keep seeking inspiration until I finally have my sign.

3.   I Am Open-Minded

I understand that my learning and ability to grow would be massively compromised if I was anything other than open-minded. I am open to influence from any person or any source at any time in the knowledge that my life could turn on a chance conversation or interaction. I realise that the world as I see it is only one perspective amongst eight billion other perspectives and that my truth is not *the* truth. This helps me to stay grounded, reflective, and introspective and puts me in the best position to learn, grow, and develop. I realise that narrow-mindedness is the enemy of progress and ultimately leads only to suffering and anxiety, so I resolve to never wander along this path.

4.   I See Money Differently than Most Other People

I look around and see that many people have a very similar attitude towards money (or lack of) and that it creates a fear in their lives. I notice that they may look for advancements in their careers so they can earn a pay raise in a job they don't necessarily enjoy or that they may fixate on their pensions so they can finally enjoy the fruits of their hard work for the last ten or twenty years of their life. I find this approach mystifying because I know there is another way, one that can give me financial freedom earlier as well as fulfilment. I understand that society aims to limit people's expectations of what they can do in their lives, including how wealthy they can be, and that these limitations affect many individuals. I, however, am not one of them.

5.   I Understand That the World Owes Me Nothing

I see entitlement as a vehicle only for selfishness, narcissism, vanity, and laziness—none of which are traits that will help me achieve what I want to achieve in my life. Instead, I embrace personal values that I have worked hard to identify. I know that responsibility for my own life means being of service to others and expecting nothing in return. It also means owning my failures as well as my successes. If something goes wrong, I realise that blaming other people or my situation is not only disingenuous but also harmful to my soul. Instead, when something does go wrong or I have an obstacle to overcome, I do it with a renewed sense of optimism and determination.

6. I Embrace and Welcome Risk

I realise that taking risks is a crucial part of reaching my potential and that trying to create safety in my life will only create a claustrophobic and stifling experience. I am clever enough to weigh up the risk involved in taking a big decision, but if my head and heart tell me that it is right for me, I have the courage to take action. I observe the risk-averse nature of many in society and see that being fearful and not committing to risk more often than not gives rise to feelings of boredom, frustration, and even despair. I am aware that the zeitgeist of the times is one of safety and security, but for me, this just won't do. I want to build a more wholesome character and a more bountiful life, and this entails an element of risk. I understand that the risk associated with staying where I am in my life is greater than the risk associated with me changing my life.

7. My Opinion Often Clashes with the Majority

This used to frustrate me and sometimes still does, but now I see it as a valuable attribute. I have a deeper understanding of myself and the world through reading, travel, learning, and deep reflection. This gives me the ability to be able to spot the huge flaws in widely accepted views and to laugh in the face of much conventional wisdom. I see orthodoxy, groupthink, and a powerful herd mentality all around me in life, and I observe a tendency for people to be afraid to be the one who thinks, let alone acts, on a completely different trajectory. Authenticity and honesty, rather than conformity or sycophancy, are my very essence.

8.　I Believe I Have a Deeper Purpose in Life

I want to make a major positive impact on the world. I have an acute realisation that the time left in my life is ebbing away, and for this reason, I want to make a promise to myself to use my time wisely and to be the best possible person that I can be. I want to serve others, help them find the meaning they so desperately want in their lives, and in the process understand myself more and more each day. I want the gift that I create, as well as myself as a person, to leave a legacy.

9.　I Am Resourceful

I realise that life is a series of challenges that must be met with resolve and resourcefulness. This does not faze me and instead fills me with resolve. I embrace learning, tap into whoever or whatever I can lean on for support, and most importantly take action.

10. I Deal with Adversity

I am wise enough to understand that adversity forms a key part of my mission in life and that, without suffering, I know I cannot grow. In fact, I have already dealt with adversity in my life, which has brought me to many realisations and prepared me for my next step. I know that dealing with things when times are hard gives me a deeper understanding of myself than is possible when everything in my life is in flow. I know that the experience gained through dealing with sadness, depression, negativity, or anything else will help me in my future and help me to help others who may be struggling. I know I can cope with anything that life presents to me. My experience in dealing with negativity and adversity has also given me the confidence to let go of the people in my life who bring bad feeling, and instead I put more energy into my positive and fruitful relationships.

11. I Identify Limiting Beliefs and Eliminate Them

I observe the voice in my head that tells me that I am not good enough, but I try not to pay attention to it. I have the awareness to not be sabotaged by negative patterns of thinking and have developed ways to replace negative thoughts with positive ones, as challenging as this is. I have also developed the skills to identify what beliefs I have that don't serve me and seek to eliminate them or reframe them. I once looked at self-doubt as a burden. I now see it as an integral part of who I am because it means I am constantly questioning and staying grounded. I was once afraid of admitting my mistakes, whereas now I recast every mistake or failure as a success because I have learned something new as an outcome. I once thought I couldn't be wealthy or even deserved to be wealthy, and I now see this belief as utter nonsense. Whatever limiting beliefs I have, I am brave enough to challenge my existing views and preconceptions to ensure that my beliefs serve, rather than inhibit me.

12. I Choose Not to Be Negatively Affected by People Who Are Suspicious of Me or Tell Me I Am Misguided

I want to be a student and a teacher each day for the rest of my life. People around me have noticed a massive change as I prepare and then embark on a whole new journey in my life. I have been told that am not destined to be a success, that I am wasting my time and money, or that I haven't seriously considered the consequences of my decisions. I am present enough to understand that for some, their fears arise from a loving place, and they are trying to protect me; for others, they are simply bitter and resentful. While it may be frustrating, I listen in the full knowledge that absolutely nothing is going to stop me from pursuing my own path.

The Truth Does Not Exist

This book contains my story, my observations, and my opinion, but one thing it does not contain is *the* truth. This is important to remember in our confused world because just as we must be on guard against being fooled by a malevolent lie, we must also be vigilant that we are not driven to madness in a fanatical pursuit of *the* truth. Instead, we must remember that truth is personal and ever evolving. Our truth lies in how we interact with the world, how we present ourselves to others, and how we seek to tap into our intuition. It is how we interpret what we read and hear about current events, our country, our culture, and our history and how we use this information to shape our own perceptions and therefore our behaviour. It is in an appreciation of the human condition and in an understanding of our flawed and deeply imperfect nature. It is shaped by our travels, our relationship with nature, and our associations with others. It is revealed in how open we are to questioning our ideas, expanding and opening our minds, and reflecting on our own psyche, character, and beliefs. It is shown in our approach towards risk and our understanding of what scares us and why. It is unearthed in how we see ourselves fitting into society and how much responsibility we wish to take in shaping that society. For me, the best manifestation of what at this present moment is my truth lies in the form of this book. What is your truth?

The Choice
Truth and Light

Now is the Time to Choose a Side

I hope that this book has emboldened you and that it has clarified for you what it is you can do to help wrestle back control from the ideologues, psychopaths, sycophants, and fools and tip the scales back towards freedom. In essence, the solution to ending tyranny and creating a better society that is genuinely fairer, cherishes diversity of thought, respects individual rights, protects children and old people, and values freedom and truth is simple. It really relies on one thing: How much responsibility are *you* willing to take? This entails examining how comfortable you are in taking orders on how to live your life from those who have no right to do so, deciding which rules you must disobey, resolving to stand up and voice your concerns when you see that something is patently wrong, summoning up the courage to step into the fear and uncertainty to do what is right and defend and protect with everything you have those values of democracy, bodily autonomy, individualism, and freedom of speech and expression for the next generation.

Only seventy-five years ago, my grandparents did exactly this. One grandfather fought valiantly in North Africa against enemy forces, and the other was on the beach at Dunkirk in 1940, later remarking that his overriding memory was the smell of burning human flesh. Meanwhile, my grandmothers faced the might of the Nazi air force during the Liverpool Blitz but stood strong and stoically as the bombs rained down on them. It has been said many times before, but their sacrifice for us was magnificent and selfless. What maybe hasn't been said is that the fact we have let totalitarianism wash up on our shores a mere two generations later is unforgivable.

For what, if not to banish the terror of tyranny for many years, did millions of men and women give their lives? Our complacency has been staggering; our cowardice even more so. But all, as I have passionately tried to argue in this book, is not lost, for just as it takes the consent of millions to enable tyrannical rule, those same people can remove their consent whenever they want. That is, if they want.

The only question that remains is this: How much do you love your freedom? To answer, you must now choose a side. It's worth remembering what is at stake for all of us. We are dealing with an enemy that is intent on destroying everything that the West once held dear, that we all held dear. This enemy wants to remove the right to free speech entirely so it can usher in a new world completely devoid of truth. It detests the resourceful and community spirited nature of small business and is intent on obliterating all of them. It hates the concepts of nationhood, family, patriotism, and tradition so they must be vilified, attacked, and broken to pieces. It views old people as a burden on the state, unworthy of life, and able to be sacrificed whenever required. It sees children as nothing more than political weapons and medical guinea pigs, to be used in any way that will further the cause for the Brave New World. It sees art, music, and comedy as expressions of creativity and ingenuity, and they are thus to be hollowed out, sanitised, and brutally censored. It recognises that history is the best possible way for a nation to understand itself, so history must be rewritten and recast so as to undermine, confuse, and demoralise the citizens. It detests the ideas of community, cooperation, and conversation and so will use its ill-gotten power to further isolate each individual from every other individual. It is misanthropic in the extreme and will stop at nothing to confuse and intimidate until it breaks the will of each and every man, woman, and child. It is extreme, vengeful, spiteful, and deeply resentful. It wants to control what you can do, where you can go, whom you can be with, what you can own, and what choices you can make for your own health and the health of your children. It despises humanity to such an extent that it will stop at nothing to impose its rancid, vicious, evil vision on all of us.

It will ensure that war will be peace, freedom will be slavery, and ignorance will be strength.

For years, this enemy insidiously wrapped itself around the sphere of society, presenting itself as a force for respect, tolerance, kindness, openness, and equality whilst overtly demonstrating that it stood for the opposite of all of these things. A society that largely was respectful, tolerant, kind, open, and equitable naively did little to resist its wickedness. With ruthless intention and growing its poisonous influence with each passing day, it began to infiltrate all organisational structures and capture the media and political narrative. Society continued to stand by as the old world, based on fundamental values of decency, humility, and openness, began to melt away. And now this enemy has a level of control on our lives that should strike terror into anybody paying even the vaguest level of attention.

This book will be dismissed by the useful idiots doing the bidding of evil forces and the fools drunk on their own ignorance and moral vanity as hate literature or an intolerant alt-right rag. As sure as the tide rises and falls, I know that will happen. They will have nothing to offer other than unbridled vitriol and venom. And yet it doesn't bother me, because despicable zealots pushing evil ideology on our world deserve neither my nor anybody else's attention or respect. These messengers of malevolence, hatred, and division may appear influential, but that is because we allow them to be. They are small in number, yet they shout the loudest and are relentless, so consumed they are by their own self-loathing and disgust for humanity. It is incumbent on each of us to face down these repugnant individuals by standing up for what we know to be right, by not being cowed by their aggressive rhetoric, and by vehemently defending our right to have an opinion and to be heard.

But this is not enough, for even more must be done by those of us who can see the enemy, as well as read its intentions. We must remember that once we can see, we cannot unsee, and therefore we have a responsibility to act. To stay on the fence at this late stage *is* to choose a side—the side of tyranny, suffering, and a future of darkness and dread. Instead, we must stand firm; call out the evil as and when it presents itself in all of its various guises; take on the ideologues with wit, passion, creativity, imagination, and dignity; defend what is left of our values; and, through our own individual attributes and with resolve and courage, begin bit by bit to rebuild a society that is one that future generations can enjoy and will thank us for gifting them. In these hard times, we must choose to be the strong men and women tasked with leading the way to better times.

I asked at the start of this book whether we are witnessing the sun rising on a bright new age, or the sun setting to usher in an eternal dark, cold night. The answer depends largely on this: When faced with the devil, will you slay the devil or walk into his cold embrace?

Follow The Imperfect Individual

 GETTR 

About the Author

David Coffey is a 40-year-old writer based in Lydiate, UK.

The Imperfect Individual – his first book - is based on a lifetime of insights and observations of Western society that, as he argues, has failed morally, spiritually and intellectually.

David asserts that, unless enough individuals discover or recapture their sense of purpose in life, Western civilisation will destroy itself.

David has a YouTube channel - also called The Imperfect Individual – where he explores themes relating to a rapidly changing world and the individual's place within it.

He has lived in Spain and travelled extensively around Europe and the USA.

David is a lover of nature and the great outdoors and spends much of his time walking in the countryside surrounding his home.